the cocoon collection

16 designs using Cocoon
by Marie Wallin
& Sarah Hatton

Dany

Addie

Cheri

Dory

Jeanie

Lyra Vee

Lyra Crew

Elise

Babette

Coco

Blanche Beret

Iva

Jolee

Kari

Gigi

Selene Wrap

gallery

SIZE	S	M	L	XL	XXL	
To fit bust	81-86	91-97	102-107	112-117	122-127	cm
	32-34	36-38	40-42	44-46	48-50	in

YARN
Rowan Cocoon

	9	9	10	11	11	x 100gm

(photographed in Seascape 813)

NEEDLES
1 pair 6mm (no 4) (US 10) needles & 7.00mm (no 2) (US K10½) crochet hook

TENSION
3 patt reps to 14 cm and 5 rows to 10 cm measured over patt using 7.00mm (US K10 ½) hook.

UK CROCHET ABBREVIATIONS
ch = chain; **dc** = double crochet; **tr** = treble; **dtr** = double treble; **sp** = space.

BACK and FRONT (both alike)
Using 6mm (US 10) needles cast on 58 [66: 74: 82: 94] sts.
Row 1 (RS): K2, *P2, K2, rep from * to end.
Row 2: P2, *K2, P2, rep from * to end.
These 2 rows form rib.
Work in rib for a further 17 rows, ending with **WS** facing for next row.
Cast off in rib (on **WS**) but do **NOT** fasten off.
Slip rem loop onto 7.00mm (US K10½) hook and work across cast-off edge as folls:
Row 1 (RS): 1 ch (does NOT count as st), 1 dc into each of first 4 [7: 5: 4: 9] cast-off sts, 2 dc into next cast-off st, (1 dc into each of next 11 [16: 6: 8: 24] cast-off sts, 2 dc into next cast-off st) 4 [3: 9: 8: 3] times, 1 dc into each of last 5 [7: 5: 5: 9] cast-off sts, turn. 63 [70: 84: 91: 98] sts.
Row 2: 1 ch (does NOT count as st), 1 dc into each dc to end, turn.
Row 3: 4 ch (counts as first tr and 1 ch), 1 tr into dc at base of 4 ch, *2 ch, miss 5 dc, 4 tr into next dc**, 2 ch, 1 tr into next dc, rep from * to end, ending last rep at **, turn.
Row 4: 4 ch (counts as first tr and 1 ch), 1 tr into tr at base of 4 ch, 2 ch, miss (3 tr, 2 ch and 1 tr), *(4 tr, 2 ch and 1 tr) into next ch sp, 2 ch, miss (4 tr, 2 ch and 1 tr), rep from * to last ch sp, 4 tr into last ch sp, turn. 9 [10: 12: 13: 14] patt reps.
(**Note**: When working foll 2 rows, work the first 3 ch at the beg of each row **loosely** so that row-end edges are not too tight.)
Row 5: 4 ch (counts as first dtr), (3 tr, 2 ch and 1 tr) into tr at base of 4 ch – ½ patt rep increased, 2 ch, miss (3 tr, 2 ch and 1 tr), *(4 tr,

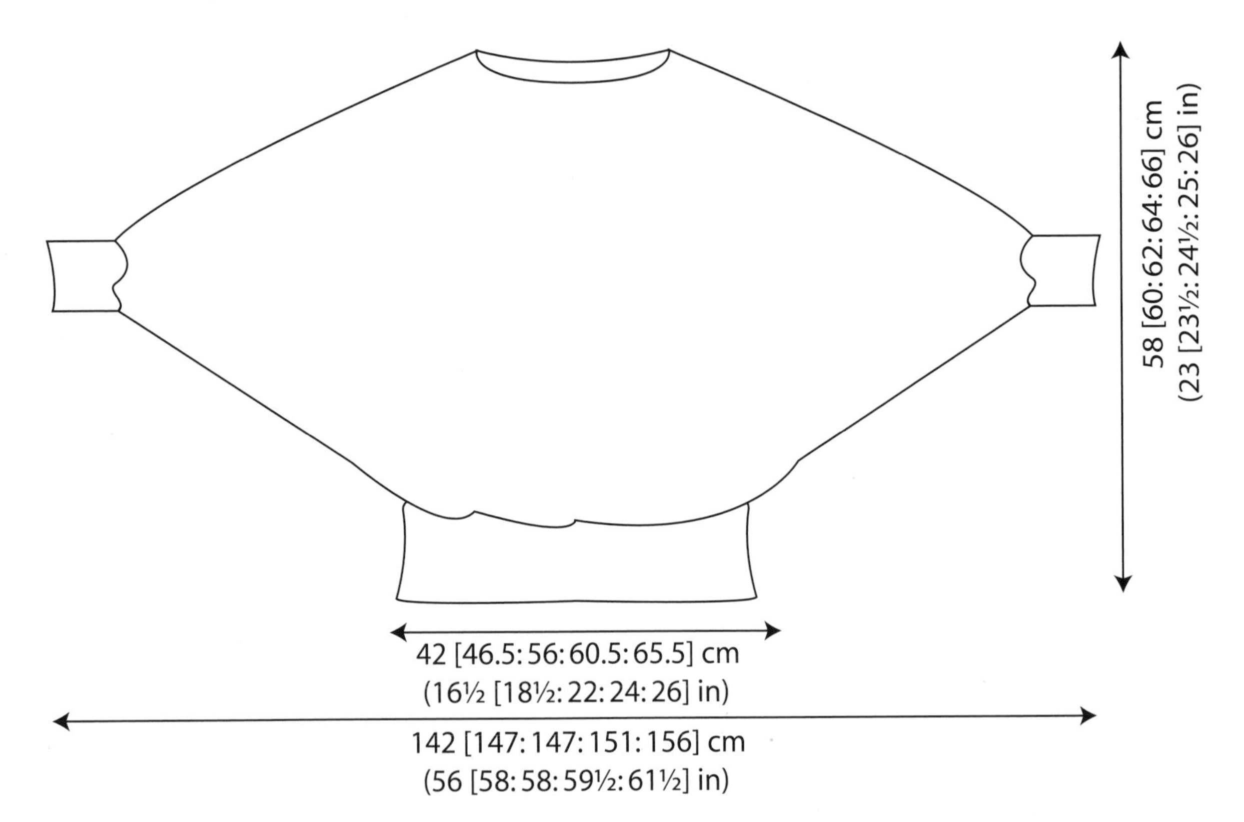

2 ch and 1 tr) into next ch sp, 2 ch, miss (4 tr, 2 ch and 1 tr), rep from ★ to last ch sp, (4 tr, 2 ch and 1 dtr) into last ch sp – 1/2 patt rep increased, turn.

Row 6: 5 ch (counts as first dtr and 1 ch), 1 tr into dtr at base of 5 ch, 2 ch, (4 tr, 2 ch and 1 tr) into first ch sp – 1/2 patt rep increased, ★2 ch, miss (4 tr, 2 ch and 1 tr), (4 tr, 2 ch and 1 tr) into next ch sp, rep from ★ until (4 tr, 2 ch and 1 tr) have been worked into last ch sp, 2 ch, miss 3 tr, (3 tr and 1 dtr) into top of 4 ch at beg of previous row – 1/2 patt rep increased, turn.

Rep last 2 rows 8 [8: 7: 7: 7] times more. 27 [28: 28: 29: 30] patt reps.

Next row (RS): 4 ch (counts as first tr and 1 ch), 1 tr into dtr at base of 4 ch, 2 ch, miss (3 tr, 2 ch and 1 tr), ★(4 tr, 2 ch and 1 tr) into next ch sp, 2 ch, miss (4 tr, 2 ch and 1 tr), rep from ★ to last ch sp, 4 tr into last ch sp, turn.

Next row: 4 ch (counts as first tr and 1 ch), 1 tr into tr at base of 4 ch, 2 ch, miss (3 tr, 2 ch and 1 tr), ★(4 tr, 2 ch and 1 tr) into next ch sp, 2 ch, miss (4 tr, 2 ch and 1 tr), rep from ★ to last ch sp, 4 tr into last ch sp, turn.

Rep last row until work meas approx 58 [60: 62: 64: 66] cm from cast-on edge, ending with RS facing for next row.

Fasten off.

MAKING UP

Press as described on the information page.

Join top of last row of back to top of last row of front to form shoulder/overarm seams, leaving 22 [22: 23: 23: 24] cm open at centre for neck opening. Mark points along row-end edges 12 [12: 13: 13: 14] cm either side of shoulder/overarm seams.

Cuffs (both alike)

With RS facing and using 6mm (US 10) needles, pick up and knit 34 [34: 38: 38: 42] sts evenly along row-end edges between marked points.

Beg with row 2, work in rib as given for back and front until cuff meas 8 cm from pick-up row, ending with RS facing for next row.

Cast off in rib.

See information page for finishing instructions.

SIZE

	S	M	L	XL	XXL	
To fit bust						
	81-86	91-97	102-107	112-117	122-127	cm
	32-34	36-38	40-42	44-46	48-50	in

YARN
Rowan Cocoon

7	8	9	10	11	x 100gm

(photographed in Emerald 814)

NEEDLES
1 pair 6mm (no 4) (US 10) needles
1 pair 7mm (no 2) (US 10½) needles
6mm (no 4) (US 10) circular needle

BUTTONS – 1 x 00421

TENSION
14 sts and 20 rows to 10 cm measured over patt using 7mm (US 10½) needles.

BACK
Using 7mm (US 10½) needles cast on 66 [72: 82: 90: 100] sts.
Row 1 (RS): P0 [1: 0: 0: 0], K0 [2: 0: 0: 1], *P2, K2, rep from * to last 2 [1: 2: 2: 3] sts, P2 [1: 2: 2: 2], K0 [0: 0: 0: 1].
Row 2: K0 [1: 0: 0: 0], P0 [2: 0: 0: 1], *K2, P2, rep from * to last 2 [1: 2: 2: 3] sts, K2 [1: 2: 2: 2], P0 [0: 0: 0: 1].
Row 3: As row 2.
Row 4: As row 1.
These 4 rows form patt.
Cont in patt until back meas 35 [36: 37: 38: 39] cm, ending with RS facing for next row.
Shape armholes
Keeping patt correct, cast off 3 sts at beg of next 2 rows.
60 [66: 76: 84: 94] sts.
Dec 1 st at each end of next 3 [3: 5: 7: 9] rows, then on foll 2 [3: 4: 4: 5] alt rows. 50 [54: 58: 62: 66] sts.
Cont straight until armhole meas 18 [19: 20: 21: 22] cm, ending with RS facing for next row.
Shape shoulders and back neck
Cast off 4 [4: 5: 5: 6] sts at beg of next 2 rows. 42 [46: 48: 52: 54] sts.
Next row (RS): Cast off 4 [4: 5: 5: 6] sts, patt until there are 6 [8: 7: 9: 9] sts on right needle and turn, leaving rem sts on a holder.
Work each side of neck separately.
Cast off 3 sts at beg of next row.
Cast off rem 3 [5: 4: 6: 6] sts.
With RS facing, rejoin yarn to rem sts, cast off centre 22 [22: 24: 24: 24] sts, patt to end.
Complete to match first side, reversing shapings.

LEFT FRONT
Using 7mm (US 10½) needles cast on 8 [11: 16: 20: 25] sts.
Row 1 (RS): P0 [1: 0: 0: 0], K0 [2: 0: 0: 1], (P2, K2) 2 [2: 4: 5: 6] times.
Row 2: Inc in first st, P1, (K2, P2) 1 [2: 3: 4: 5] times, K2 [1: 2: 2: 2], P0 [0: 0: 0: 1].
Row 3: K0 [1: 0: 0: 0], P0 [2: 0: 0: 1], (K2, P2) 2 [2: 4: 5: 6] times, inc in last st.
Row 4: Inc in first st, P1, K2, (P2, K2) 1 [2: 3: 4: 5] times, P2 [1: 2: 2: 2], K0 [0: 0: 0: 1]. 11 [14: 19: 23: 28] sts.
These 4 rows form patt and beg front shaping.
Inc 1 st at end of next row and at same edge on foll 6 rows, then on foll 4 alt rows, then on 3 foll 4th rows, then on 2 foll 6th rows, then on 2 foll 8th rows, taking inc sts into patt.
29 [32: 37: 41: 46] sts.
Cont straight until left front matches back to beg of armhole shaping, ending with RS facing for next row.
Shape armhole
Keeping patt correct, cast off 3 sts at beg of next row.
26 [29: 34: 38: 43] sts.
Work 1 row.
Dec 1 st at armhole edge of next 3 [3: 5: 7: 9] rows, then on foll 2 [3: 3: 3: 3] alt rows. 21 [23: 26: 28: 31] sts.
Work 2 [2: 0: 0: 0] rows, ending with **WS** facing for next row.
Shape neck
Keeping patt correct, cast off 3 [3: 4: 4: 4] sts at beg of next row.
18 [20: 22: 24: 27] sts.
Dec 1 st at neck edge of next 4 rows, then on foll 2 alt rows, then on foll 4th row **and at same time** dec 0 [0: 1: 1: 1] st at armhole edge of 0 [0: next: next: next] and foll 0 [0: 0: 0: 1] alt row.
11 [13: 14: 16: 18] sts.
Cont straight until left front matches back to beg of shoulder shaping, ending with RS facing for next row.
Shape shoulder
Cast off 4 [4: 5: 5: 6] sts at beg of next and foll alt row.
Work 1 row.
Cast off rem 3 [5: 4: 6: 6] sts.

RIGHT FRONT
Using 7mm (US 10½) needles cast on 8 [11: 16: 20: 25] sts.

Row 1 (RS): K2, (P2, K2) 1 [2: 3: 4: 5] times, P2 [1: 2: 2: 2], K0 [0: 0: 0: 1].
Row 2: K0 [1: 0: 0: 0], P0 [2: 0: 0: 1], (K2, P2) 1 [1: 3: 4: 5] times, K2, P1, inc in last st.
Row 3: Inc in first st, P2, (K2, P2) 1 [2: 3: 4: 5] times, K2 [1: 2: 2: 2], P0 [0: 0: 0: 1].
Row 4: P0 [1: 0: 0: 0], K0 [2: 0: 0: 1], (P2, K2) 2 [2: 4: 5: 6] times, P1, inc in last st. 11 [14: 19: 23: 28] sts.
These 4 rows form patt and beg front shaping.
Complete to match left front, reversing shapings.

SLEEVES
Using 6mm (US 10) needles cast on 30 [32: 34: 34: 36] sts.
Row 1 (RS): K0 [0: 0: 0: 1], P0 [1: 2: 2: 2], *K2, P2, rep from * to last 2 [3: 0: 0: 1] sts, K2 [2: 0: 0: 1], P0 [1: 0: 0: 0].
Row 2: P0 [0: 0: 0: 1], K0 [1: 2: 2: 2], *P2, K2, rep from * to last 2 [3: 0: 0: 1] sts, P2 [2: 0: 0: 1], K0 [1: 0: 0: 0].
These 2 rows form rib.
Work in rib for a further 12 rows, ending with RS facing for next row.
Change to 7mm (US 10½) needles.
Now work in patt as folls:
Row 1 (RS): P0 [0: 0: 0: 1], K0 [1: 2: 2: 2], *P2, K2, rep from * to last 2 [3: 0: 0: 1] sts, P2 [2: 0: 0: 1], K0 [1: 0: 0: 0].
Row 2: K0 [0: 0: 0: 1], P0 [1: 2: 2: 2], *K2, P2, rep from * to last 2 [3: 0: 0: 1] sts, K2 [2: 0: 0: 1], P0 [1: 0: 0: 0].
Row 3: As row 2.
Row 4: As row 1.
These 4 rows form patt.
Cont in patt, shaping sides by inc 1 st at each end of next and every foll 6th row to 46 [46: 46: 54: 56] sts, then on every foll 8th row until there are 50 [52: 54: 56: 58] sts, taking inc sts into patt.
Cont straight until sleeve meas 46 [47: 48: 48: 48] cm, ending with RS facing for next row.
Shape top
Keeping patt correct, cast off 3 sts at beg of next 2 rows.
44 [46: 48: 50: 52] sts.
Dec 1 st at each end of next 3 rows, then on every foll alt row until 22 sts rem, then on foll 5 rows, ending with RS facing for next row.
Cast off rem 12 sts.

MAKING UP
Press as described on the information page.
Join both shoulder seams using back stitch, or mattress stitch if preferred.
Neckband
With RS facing and using 6mm (US 10) needles, beg and ending at front opening edges, pick up and knit 28 [28: 31: 31: 33] sts up right side of neck, 28 [28: 30: 30: 30] sts from back, then 28 [28: 31: 31: 33] sts down left side of neck. 84 [84: 92: 92: 96] sts.
Row 1 (WS): K1, P2, *K2, P2, rep from * to last st, K1.
Row 2: K3, *P2, K2, rep from * to last st, K1.
These 2 rows form rib.
Cont in rib for a further 8 rows, ending with **WS** facing for next row.
Cast off in rib (on **WS**).
Join both side seams.
Front and hem band
With RS facing and using 6mm (US 10) circular needle, beg and ending at top of neckband, pick up and knit 28 [32: 34: 36: 40] sts down left front opening edge to last inc, 59 sts down left front shaped row-end edge to cast-on edge, 8 [11: 16: 20: 25] sts from left front cast-on edge, 66 [72: 82: 90: 100] sts from back cast-on edge, 8 [11: 16: 20: 25] sts from right front cast-on edge, 59 sts up right front shaped row-end edge to last inc, then 28 [32: 34: 36: 40] sts up right front opening edge. 256 [276: 300: 320: 348] sts.
Beg with row 1, work in rib as given for neckband for 4 rows, ending with **WS** facing for next row.
Row 5 (WS): Rib 3, cast off 2 sts (to make a buttonhole – cast on 2 sts over these cast-off sts on next row), rib to end.
Cont in rib for a further 5 rows, ending with **WS** facing for next row.
Cast off in rib (on **WS**).
See information page for finishing instructions, setting in sleeves using the set-in method.

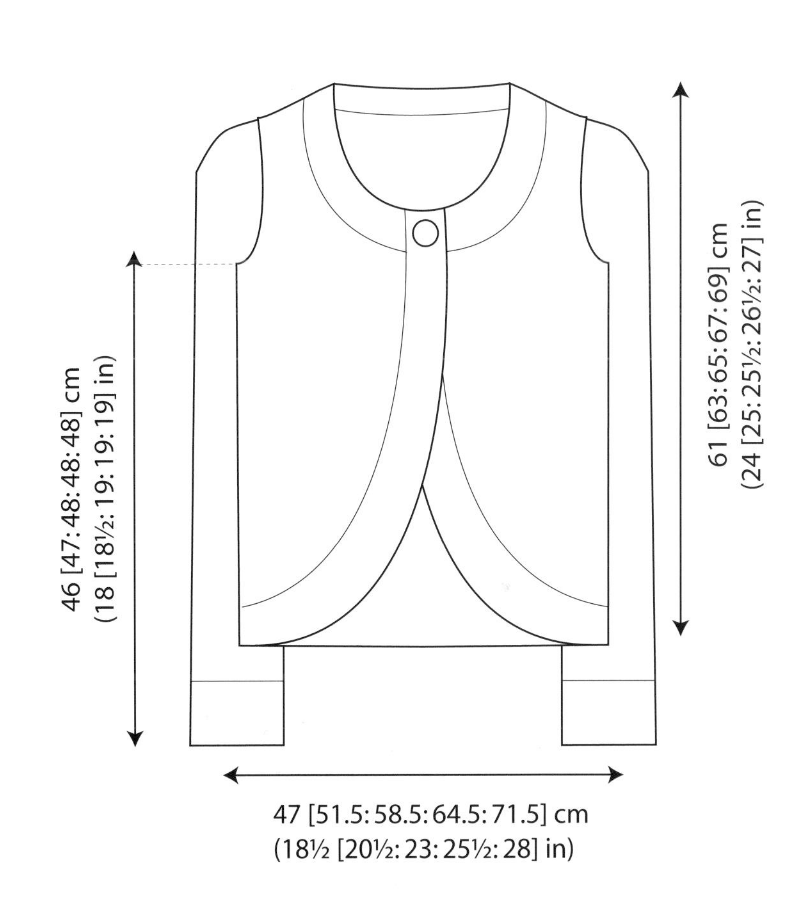

SIZE

	S	M	L	XL	XXL	
To fit bust						
	81-86	91-97	102-107	112-117	122-127	cm
	32-34	36-38	40-42	44-46	48-50	in

YARN
Rowan Cocoon

6	6	7	8	9	x 100gm

(photographed in Lavender Ice 811)

NEEDLES
1 pair 6mm (no 4) (US 10) needles
1 pair 7mm (no 2) (US 10½) needles
1 pair 8mm (no 0) (US 11) needles

TENSION
15 sts and 18 rows to 10 cm measured over pattern using 7mm (US 10½) needles.

BACK
Using 6mm (US 10) needles cast on 74 [82: 90: 102: 110] sts.
Row 1 (RS): K2, *P2, K2, rep from * to end.
Row 2: P2, *K2, P2, rep from * to end.
These 2 rows form rib.
Work in rib for a further 9 rows, - [inc: inc: dec: -] – [1: 2: 1: -] sts evenly across last row and ending with **WS** facing for next row.
74 [83: 92: 101: 110] sts.
Change to 7mm (US 10½) needles.
Cont in lace patt as folls:
Row 1 (WS): Purl.
Row 2: K2, *yfwd, K2, sl 1, K1, psso, K2tog, K2, yfwd, K1, rep from * to end.
Row 3: Purl.
Row 4: K1, *yfwd, K2, sl 1, K1, psso, K2tog, K2, yfwd, K1, rep from * to last st, K1.
These 4 rows form patt.
Cont in patt until back meas 34 [35: 36: 37: 38] cm, ending with RS facing for next row.
Place markers at both ends of last row to denote base of armholes.
Cont straight until armhole meas 24 [25: 26: 27: 28] cm, ending with RS facing for next row.
Shape shoulders and back neck
Cast off 7 [8: 10: 11: 12] sts at beg of next 2 rows.
60 [67: 72: 79: 86] sts.
Next row (RS): Cast off 7 [8: 10: 11: 12] sts, patt until there are 10 [12: 12: 14: 16] sts on right needle and turn, leaving rem sts on a holder.
Work each side of neck separately.
Cast off 3 sts at beg of next row.
Cast off rem 7 [9: 9: 11: 13] sts.
With RS facing, rejoin yarn to rem sts, cast off centre 26 [27: 28: 29: 30] sts, patt to end.
Complete to match first side, reversing shapings.

FRONT
Work as given for back until 18 [18: 20: 20: 22] rows less have been worked than on back to beg of shoulder shaping, ending with RS facing for next row.
Shape neck
Next row (RS): Patt 31 [35: 40: 44: 49] sts and turn, leaving rem sts on a holder.
Work each side of neck separately.
Keeping patt correct, dec 1 st at neck edge of next 6 rows, then on foll 4 [4: 5: 5: 6] alt rows. 21 [25: 29: 33: 37] sts.
Work 3 rows, ending with RS facing for next row.
Shape shoulder
Cast off 7 [8: 10: 11: 12] sts at beg of next and foll alt row.
Work 1 row.
Cast off rem 7 [9: 9: 11: 13] sts.
With RS facing, rejoin yarn to rem sts, cast off centre 12 [13: 12: 13: 12] sts, patt to end.
Complete to match first side, reversing shapings.

MAKING UP
Press as described on the information page.
Join right shoulder seam using back stitch, or mattress stitch if preferred.
Collar
With RS facing and using 8mm (US 11) needles, pick up and knit 19 [19: 22: 22: 22] sts down left side of neck, 13 [13: 13: 13: 12] sts from front, 19 [19: 22: 22: 22] sts up right side of neck, then 32 [32: 35: 35: 36] sts from back. 83 [83: 92: 92: 92] sts.
Row 1 (RS of collar, WS of body): Knit.
Beg with row 1, work in patt as given for back until collar meas 24 cm from pick-up row, ending with RS of collar facing for next row.
Work in g st for 3 rows, ending with **WS** of collar facing for next row.
Cast off knitwise (on **WS**).
Join left shoulder and collar seam, reversing collar seam for turn-back.

Armhole borders (both alike)
With RS facing and using 6mm (US 10) needles, pick up and knit 70 [74: 74: 78: 82] sts evenly along armhole edge between markers. Beg with row 2, work in rib as given for back, dec 1 st at each end of 2nd and foll 3 alt rows. 62 [66: 66: 70: 74] sts.
Work 1 row, ending with RS facing for next row.
Cast off in rib.
See information page for finishing instructions.

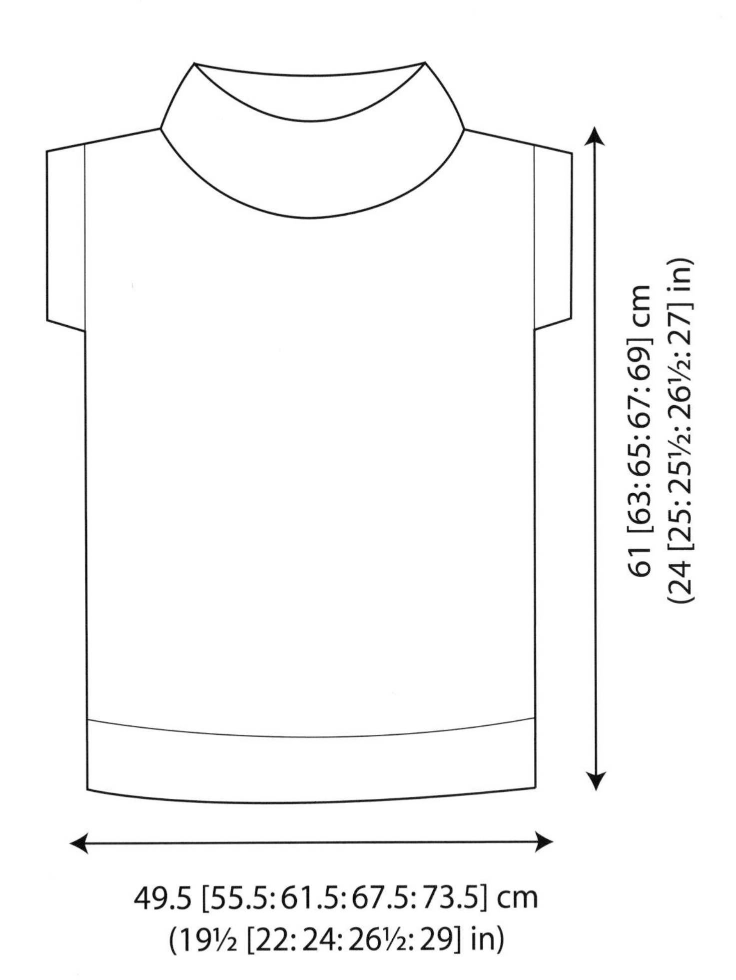

SIZE	S	M	L	XL	XXL	
To fit bust	81-86	91-97	102-107	112-117	122-127	cm
	32-34	36-38	40-42	44-46	48-50	in

YARN

Rowan Cocoon

	S	M	L	XL	XXL	
A Red Wine 819	4	5	5	6	6	x 100gm
B Quarry Tile 818	1	1	1	1	1	x 100gm
C Seascape 813	2	2	2	2	2	x 100gm
D Amber 815	1	1	2	2	2	x 100gm
E Kiwi 816	1	1	1	1	1	x 100gm

NEEDLES

1 pair 6mm (no 4) (US 10) needles & 1 pair 7mm (no 2) (US 10½) needles

TENSION

15 sts and 16½ rows to 10 cm measured over patterned st st, 14 sts and 16 rows to 10 cm measured over plain st st, both using 7mm (US 10½) needles.

BACK

Using 6mm (US 10) needles and yarn A cast on 66 [74: 82: 90: 102] sts.

Row 1 (RS): K2, *P2, K2, rep from * to end.

Row 2: P2, *K2, P2, rep from * to end.

These 2 rows form rib.

Work in rib for a further 12 rows, inc [dec: inc: inc: inc] 1 st at centre of last row and ending with RS facing for next row. 67 [73: 83: 91: 103] sts.

Change to 7mm (US 10½) needles.

Beg and ending rows as indicated, using the **fairisle** technique as described on the information page and repeating the 39 row patt rep throughout (noting that first and 3rd reps beg with a K row but 2nd rep will beg with a **P** row), now work in patt from chart, which is worked entirely in st st, as folls:

Work 4 rows, ending with RS facing for next row.

Keeping patt correct, dec 1 st at each end of next and 2 foll 4th rows. 61 [67: 77: 85: 97] sts.

Work 9 [9: 9: 11: 11] rows, ending with RS facing for next row.

Inc 1 st at each end of next and 2 foll 6th rows. 67 [73: 83: 91: 103] sts.

Cont straight until back meas 35 [36: 37: 38: 39] cm, ending with RS facing for next row.

Shape armholes

Keeping patt correct, cast off 3 sts at beg of next 2 rows. 61 [67: 77: 85: 97] sts.

Dec 1 st at each end of next 3 [3: 5: 7: 9] rows, then on foll 2 [3: 4: 4: 5] alt rows. 51 [55: 59: 63: 69] sts.

Cont straight until armhole meas 18 [19: 20: 21: 22] cm, ending with RS facing for next row.

Shape shoulders and back neck

Cast off 4 [5: 5: 6: 6] sts at beg of next 2 rows. 43 [45: 49: 51: 57] sts.

Next row (RS): Cast off 4 [5: 5: 6: 6] sts, patt until there are 7 [7: 8: 8: 10] sts on right needle and turn, leaving rem sts on a holder.

Work each side of neck separately.

Cast off 3 sts at beg of next row.

Cast off rem 4 [4: 5: 5: 7] sts.

With RS facing, rejoin yarns to rem sts, cast off centre 21 [21: 23: 23: 25] sts, patt to end.

Complete to match first side, reversing shapings.

FRONT

Work as given for back to beg of armhole shaping, ending with RS facing for next row.

Shape armholes and divide for neck

Next row (RS): Cast off 3 sts, patt until there are 29 [32: 37: 41: 47] sts on right needle and turn, leaving rem sts on a holder.

Work each side of neck separately.

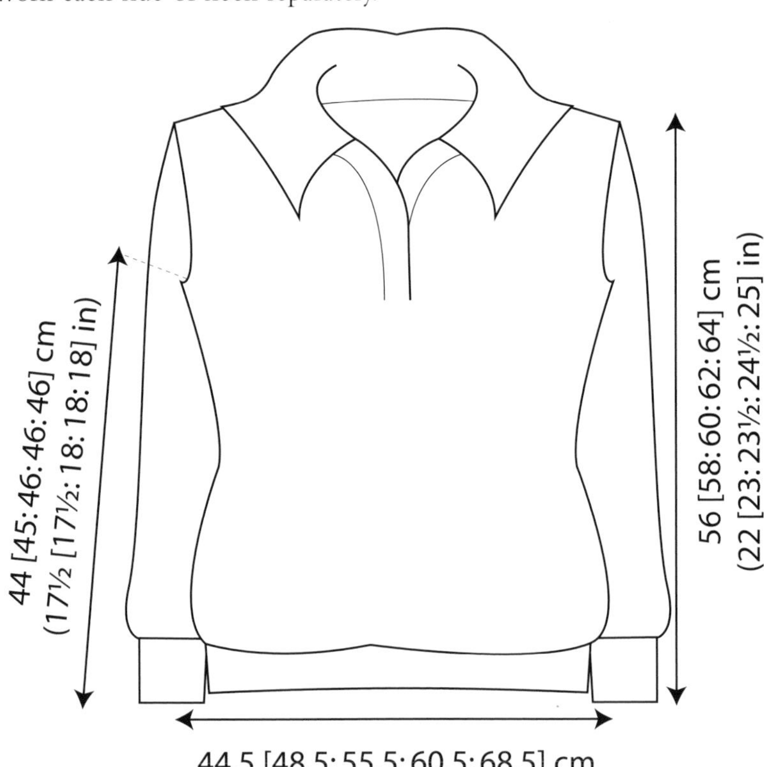

Keeping patt correct, work 1 row.
Dec 1 st at armhole edge of next 3 [3: 5: 7: 9] rows, then on foll 2 [3: 4: 4: 5] alt rows. 24 [26: 28: 30: 33] sts.
Cont straight until 8 [8: 10: 10: 12] rows less have been worked than on back to beg of shoulder shaping, ending with RS facing for next row.

Shape neck

Next row (RS): Patt to last 7 sts, cast off rem 7 sts. 17 [19: 21: 23: 26] sts.
Rejoin yarns with **WS** facing and cont as folls:
Keeping patt correct, dec 1 st at neck edge of next 4 rows, then on foll 1 [1: 2: 2: 3] alt rows. 12 [14: 15: 17: 19] sts.
Work 1 row, ending with RS facing for next row.

Shape shoulder

Cast off 4 [5: 5: 6: 6] sts at beg of next and foll alt row.
Work 1 row.
Cast off rem 4 [4: 5: 5: 7] sts.
With RS facing, rejoin yarns to rem sts, cast off centre 3 sts, patt to end.
Cast off 3 sts at beg of next row. 29 [32: 37: 41: 47] sts.
Complete to match first side, reversing shapings and working first row of neck shaping as folls:

Shape neck

Next row (RS): Cast off 7 sts, patt to end. 17 [19: 21: 23: 26] sts.

SLEEVES

Using 6mm (US 10) needles and yarn A cast on 30 sts.
Work in rib as given for back for 14 rows, dec [-: -: -: inc] 1 st at each end of last row and ending with RS facing for next row.
28 [30: 30: 30: 32] sts.
Change to 7mm (US 10½) needles.
Beg with a K row, work in st st, shaping sides by inc 1 st at each end of 3rd and foll 2 [1: 3: 5: 5] alt rows, then on every foll 4th row until there are 56 [58: 60: 62: 64] sts.
Cont straight until sleeve meas 44 [45: 46: 46: 46] cm, ending with RS facing for next row.

Shape top

Cast off 3 sts at beg of next 2 rows. 50 [52: 54: 56: 58] sts.
Dec 1 st at each end of next 5 rows, then on every foll alt row until 34 sts rem, then on foll 5 rows, ending with RS facing for next row. 24 sts.
Cast off 6 sts at beg of next 2 rows.
Cast off rem 12 sts.

MAKING UP

Press as described on the information page.
Join both shoulder seams using back stitch, or mattress stitch if preferred.

Front bands (both alike)

With RS facing, using 6mm (US 10) needles and yarn A, pick up and knit 20 [24: 24: 24: 24] sts along row-end edge of front opening, between neck shaping and cast-off sts at base of opening.
Row 1 (WS): K1, P2, *K2, P2, rep from * to last st, K1.
Row 2: K3, *P2, K2, rep from * to last st, K1.
These 2 rows form rib.
Work in rib for 1 row more, ending with RS facing for next row.
Cast off in rib.
Lay right front band over left front band and sew row-end edges to cast-off sts at base of opening.

Collar

With RS facing, using 6mm (US 10) needles and yarn A, beg and ending at cast-off edges of front bands, pick up and knit 17 [17: 19: 19: 21] sts up right side of neck, 28 [28: 30: 30: 32] sts from back, then 17 [17: 19: 19: 21] sts down left side of neck. 62 [62: 68: 68: 74] sts.
Row 1 (RS of collar, WS of body): K3, P2, *inc knitwise in next st, P2, rep from * to last 3 sts, K3. 80 [80: 88: 88: 96] sts.
Beg with row 1, work in rib as given for front bands until collar meas 8 cm from pick-up row, ending with RS of collar facing for next row.
Cast off in rib.
See information page for finishing instructions, setting in sleeves using the set-in method.

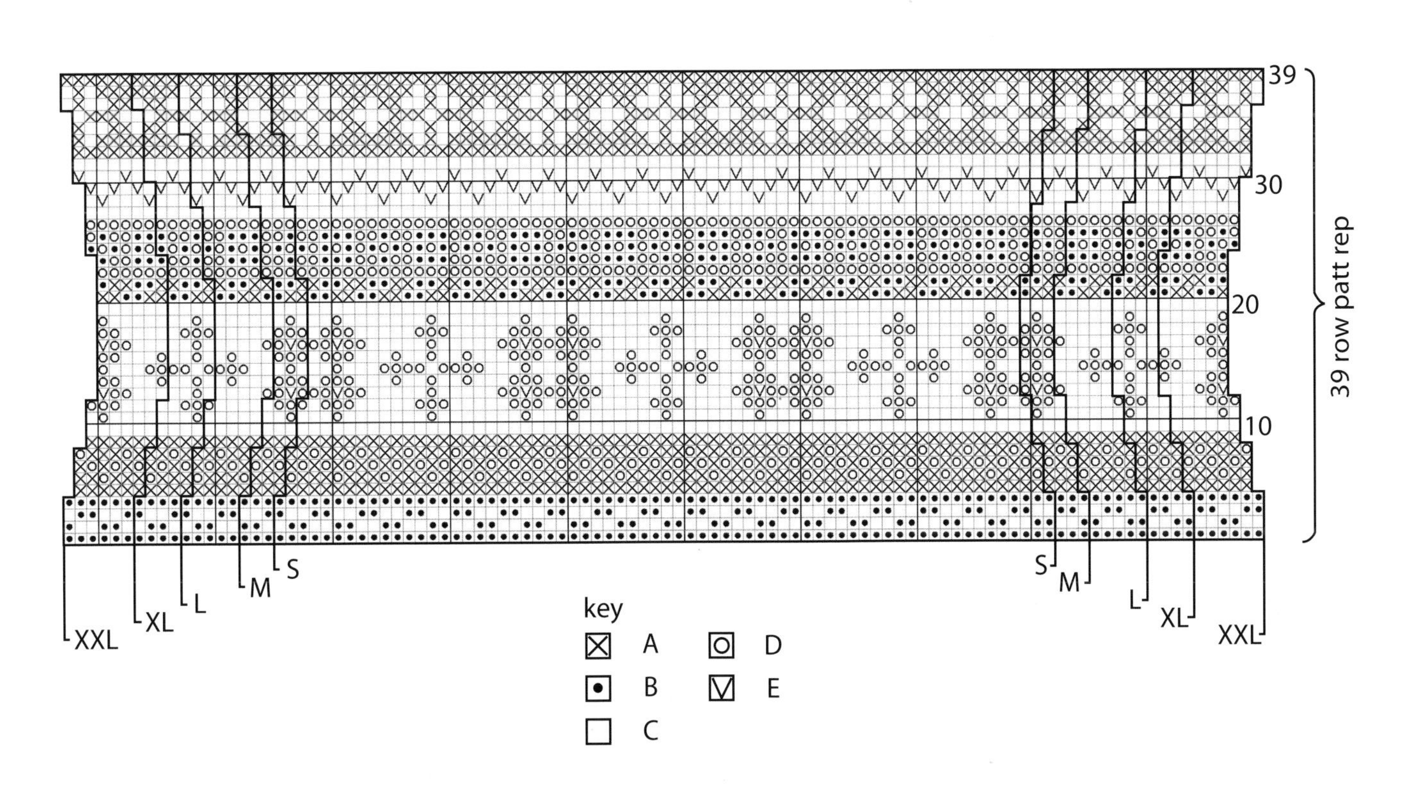

SIZE	S	M	L	XL	XXL	
To fit bust	81-86	91-97	102-107	112-117	122-127	cm
	32-34	36-38	40-42	44-46	48-50	in

YARN

Rowan Cocoon

	11	12	13	14	15	x 100gm

(photographed in Fog 820)

CROCHET HOOK

7.00mm (no 2) (US K10½) crochet hook

TENSION

12 sts and 12 rows to 10 cm measured over dc fabric using 7.00mm (US K10½) hook.

UK CROCHET ABBREVIATIONS

ch = chain; **ss** = slip stitch; **dc** = double crochet; **dc2tog** = (insert hook as indicated, yarn over hook and draw loop through) twice, yarn over hook and draw through all 3 loops; **tr** = treble; **sp** = space.

BACK

Using 7.00mm (US K10½) hook make 84 [92: 102: 114: 124] ch.

Row 1 (RS): 1 tr into 6th ch from hook, *1 ch, miss 1 ch, 1 tr into next ch, rep from * to end, turn.

Row 2: 1 ch (does NOT count as st), 1 dc into tr at base of 1 ch, *1 dc into next ch sp, 1 dc into next tr, rep from * to end, working dc at end of last rep into 4th of 5 ch at beg of previous row, turn. 81 [89: 99: 111: 121] sts.

Row 3: 1 ch (does NOT count as st), 1 dc into each dc to end, turn.

Row 4: As row 3.

These 4 rows complete border patt.

Now work in patt as folls:

Row 1 (RS): 1 ch (does NOT count as st), 1 dc into first dc, *1 ch, miss 1 dc, 1 dc into next dc, rep from * to end, turn.

Row 2: 3 ch (counts as first st), miss 1 ch sp, 1 tr into next ch sp, passing hook behind tr just worked: 1 tr into missed ch sp, *1 tr into next empty ch sp, passing hook behind tr just worked: 1 tr into previous ch sp (this already has a tr worked into it), rep from * until 2nd tr has been worked into last-but-one ch sp, 1 tr into last dc, turn.

Row 3: 1 ch (does NOT count as st), 2 dc into first tr, 1 dc into each tr to end, working last dc into top of 3 ch at beg of previous row, turn.

These 3 rows form patt.

Cont in patt until back meas approx 36 [37: 38: 39: 40] cm, ending after patt row 3.

Next row: 1 ch (does NOT count as st), 1 dc into each of first 3 [4: 3: 3: 5] dc, dc2tog over next 2 dc, (1 dc into next dc, dc2tog over next 2 dc) 24 [26: 30: 34: 36] times, 1 dc into each of last 4 [5: 4: 4: 6] dc, turn. 56 [62: 68: 76: 84] sts.

Next row: 1 ch (does NOT count as st), 1 dc into each st to end, turn.

Last row forms dc fabric.

Cont in dc fabric until back meas 41 [42: 43: 44: 45] cm.

Shape armholes

Next row: ss across and into 4th st, 1 ch (does NOT count as st), 1 dc into dc at base of 1 ch (this is same dc as used for last ss) – 3 sts decreased, 1 dc into each dc to last 3 dc and turn, leaving rem 3 dc unworked – 3 sts decreased. 50 [56: 62: 70: 78] sts.

Next row: 1 ch (does NOT count as st), dc2tog over first 2 sts – 1 st decreased, 1 dc into each dc to last 2 sts, dc2tog over last 2 sts – 1 st decreased, turn.

Working all decreases as set by last row, dec 1 st at each end of next 2 [4: 5: 8: 9] rows. 44 [46: 50: 52: 58] sts.

Cont straight until armhole meas 19 [20: 21: 22: 23] cm.

Shape back neck

Next row (RS): 1 ch (does NOT count as st), 1 dc into each of first 12 [13: 15: 16: 18] dc and turn, leaving rem sts unworked.

Dec 1 st at neck edge of next row. 11 [12: 14: 15: 17] sts.

Shape shoulder

Fasten off.

Return to last complete row worked, miss centre 20 [20: 20: 20: 22] sts, rejoin yarn to next dc, 1 ch (does NOT count as st), 1 dc into same dc as where yarn was rejoined, 1 dc into each dc to end, turn.

Dec 1 st at neck edge of next row. 11 [12: 14: 15: 17] sts.

Shape shoulder

Fasten off.

LEFT FRONT

Using 7.00mm (US K10 1/2) hook make 40 [44: 48: 54: 60] ch.

Work the 4 border patt rows as given for back. 37 [41: 45: 51: 57] sts.

Now work in patt as given for back until left front meas approx 36 [37: 38: 39: 40] cm, ending after patt row 3.

Next row: 1 ch (does NOT count as st), 1 dc into each of first 1 [1: 2: 2: 2] dc, dc2tog over next 2 dc, (1 dc into next dc, dc2tog over next 2 dc) 11 [12: 13: 15: 17] times, 1 dc into each of last 1 [2: 2: 2: 2] dc, turn. 25 [28: 31: 35: 39] sts.

Cont in dc fabric as given for back until left front matches back to beg of armhole shaping.

Shape armhole

Working all shaping as set by back, dec 3 sts at armhole edge of next row, then 1 st at armhole edge of foll 3 [5: 6: 9: 10] rows. 19 [20: 22: 23: 26] sts.

Cont straight until 10 [10: 11: 11: 12] rows less have been worked than on back to shoulder fasten-off.

Shape neck

Working all shaping as set by armholes, dec 3 sts at front opening (neck) edge of next row, then 1 st at neck edge of next 3 [3: 2: 2: 3] rows, then on foll 2 [2: 3: 3: 3] alt rows. 11 [12: 14: 15: 17] sts.

Work 2 rows.

Shape shoulder

Fasten off.

RIGHT FRONT

Work as given for left front, reversing shapings.

SLEEVES

Using 7.00mm (US K10½) hook make 32 [32: 34: 34: 34] ch.

Work the 4 border patt rows as given for back. 29 [29: 31: 31: 31] sts.

Now work in patt as folls:

Row 1 (RS): 1 ch (does NOT count as st), 2 dc into first dc – 1 st increased, *1 ch, miss 1 dc**, 1 dc into next dc, rep from * to end, ending last rep at **, 2 dc into last dc – 1 st increased, turn. 31 [31: 33: 33: 33] sts.

Row 2: 3 ch (counts as first st), miss dc at base of 3 ch, 1 tr into next dc, miss 1 ch sp, 1 tr into next ch sp, passing hook behind tr just worked: 1 tr into missed ch sp, *1 tr into next empty ch sp, passing hook behind tr just worked: 1 tr into previous ch sp (this already has a tr worked into it), rep from * until 2nd tr has been worked into last-but-one ch sp, 1 tr into each of last 2 dc, turn.

Row 3: 1 ch (does NOT count as st), 2 dc into first tr, 1 dc into each tr to end, working last dc into top of 3 ch at beg of previous row, turn.

Row 4: 1 ch (does NOT count as st), 1 dc into first dc, 1 ch, 1 dc into next dc – 1 st increased, *1 ch, miss 1 dc, 1 dc into next dc, rep from * to last st, 1 ch, 1 dc into last dc – 1 st increased, turn. 33 [33: 35: 35: 35] sts.

Row 5: 3 ch (counts as first st), miss 1 ch sp, 1 tr into next ch sp, passing hook behind tr just worked: 1 tr into missed ch sp, *1 tr into next empty ch sp, passing hook behind tr just worked: 1 tr into previous ch sp (this already has a tr worked into it), rep from * until 2nd tr has been worked into last-but-one ch sp, 1 tr into last dc, turn.

Row 6: 1 ch (does NOT count as st), 2 dc into first tr, 1 dc into each tr to end, working last dc into top of 3 ch at beg of previous row, turn.

Rep these 6 rows once more. 37 [37: 39: 39: 39] sts.

Now work in dc fabric as given for back, shaping sides as folls:

Row 13: 1 ch (does NOT count as st), 2 dc into first dc – 1 st increased, 1 dc into each dc to last dc, 2 dc into last dc – 1 st increased, turn.

This row sets increases.

Cont in dc fabric, shaping sides by inc 1 st at each end of 5th [4th: 4th: 4th: 3rd] and 4 [3: 1: 6: 3] foll 5th [4th: 4th: 4th: 3rd] rows, then on – [2: 4: -: 4] foll – [5th: 5th: -: 4th] rows. 49 [51: 53: 55: 57] sts.

Cont straight until sleeve meas 45 [46: 47: 47: 47] cm.

Shape top

Working all shaping as set by armholes, dec 3 sts at each end of next row. 43 [45: 47: 49: 51] sts.

Dec 1 st at each end of next 12 [13: 14: 15: 16] rows. 19 sts.

Fasten off.

MAKING UP

Press as described on the information page.

Join both shoulder seams using back stitch, or mattress stitch if preferred.

Front bands (both alike)

With RS facing and using 7.00mm (US K10½) hook, rejoin yarn at one end of front opening edge, 1 ch (does NOT count as st), work 1 row of dc evenly along entire front opening edge, between foundation ch edge and neck shaping, ensuring an odd number of dc are worked, turn.

Work in dc fabric as given for back for 2 rows.

Next row (WS): 4 ch (counts as 1 tr and 1 ch), miss first 2 dc, 1 tr into next dc, *1 ch, miss 1 dc, 1 tr into next dc, rep from * to end.

Fasten off.

Neck edging

With RS facing and using 7.00mm (US K10½) hook, rejoin yarn at top of right front opening edge, 1 ch (does NOT count as st), work 1 row of dc evenly around entire neck edge, ending at top of left front opening edge.

Fasten off.

See information page for finishing instructions, setting in sleeves using the set-in method.

Tie

Using 7.00mm (US K10½) hook make 4 ch.

Row 1 (RS): 1 dc into 2nd ch from hook, 1 dc into each of next 2 ch, turn. 3 sts.

Row 2: 1 ch (does NOT count as st), 1 dc into each of next 3 dc, turn.

Rep last row until tie meas 150 [160: 170: 180: 190] cm.

Fasten off.

Using photograph as a guide, thread tie through last rep of patt row 2 of patt.

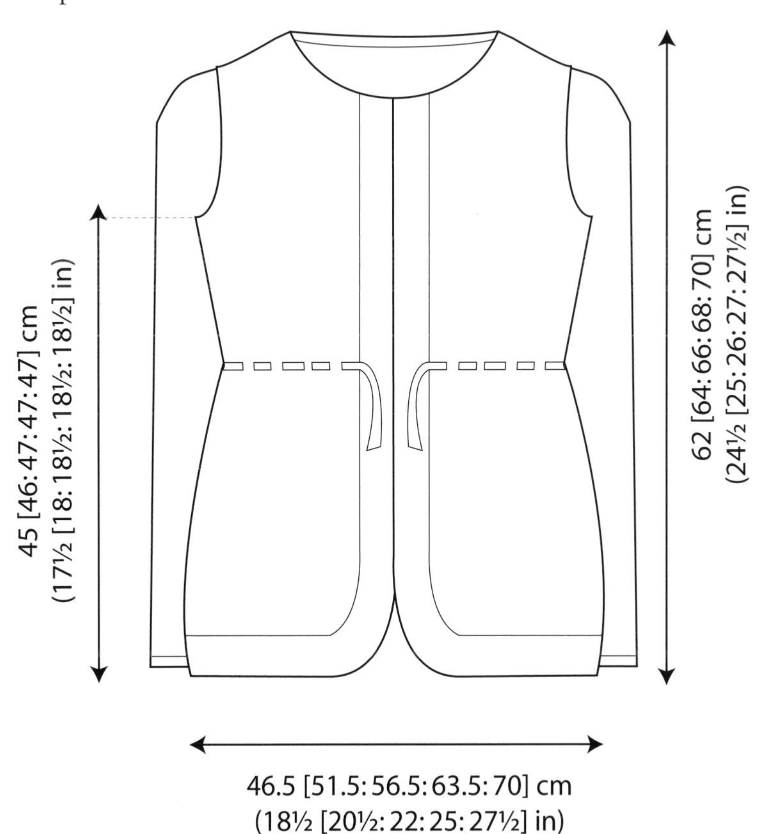

SIZE

	S	M	L	XL	
To fit bust					
	81-86	91-97	102-107	112-117	cm
	32-34	36-38	40-42	44-46	in

YARN
Rowan Cocoon

	8	9	10	11	x 100gm

(photographed in Lavender Ice 811)

NEEDLES
1 pair 6mm (no 4) (US 10) needles, 1 pair 7mm (no 2) (US 10½) needles
6mm (no 4) (US 10) circular needle & Cable needle

TENSION
14 sts and 19 rows to 10 cm measured over patt using 7mm (US 10½) needles. Cable panel (38 sts) meas 19 cm.

SPECIAL ABBREVIATIONS
C4B = slip next 2 sts onto cable needle and leave at back of work, K2, then K2 from cable needle;
C4F = slip next 2 sts onto cable needle and leave at front of work, K2, then K2 from cable needle;
Cr3L = slip next 2 sts onto cable needle and leave at front of work, P1, then K2 from cable needle;
Cr3R = slip next st onto cable needle and leave at back of work, K2, then P1 from cable needle;
Cr4L = slip next 2 sts onto cable needle and leave at front of work, P2, then K2 from cable needle;
Cr4R = slip next 2 sts onto cable needle and leave at back of work, K2, then P2 from cable needle.

BACK (worked sideways, beg at right cuff)
Using 7mm (US 10½) needles cast on 42 [44: 46: 48] sts.
Row 1 (RS): P1, K1, work next 38 sts as row 1 of chart, (K1, P1) 1 [2: 3: 4] times.
Row 2: (K1, P1) 1 [2: 3: 4] times, work next 38 sts as row 2 of chart, P1, K1.
Row 3: K1, P1, work next 38 sts as row 3 of chart, (P1, K1) 1 [2: 3: 4] times.
Row 4: (P1, K1) 1 [2: 3: 4] times, work next 38 sts as row 4 of chart, K1, P1.
These 4 rows set the sts – central cable panel with double moss st at sides.
Cont as set, shaping overarm seam by inc 1 st at beg of next and 7 foll 8th rows **and at same time** shaping underarm seam by inc 1 st at end of next and 3 [6: 7: 9] foll 4th rows, then on 8 [5: 6: 4] foll 6th rows, taking all inc sts into double moss st. 62 [64: 68: 70] sts.
Work 5 rows, ending after chart row 6 [32: 10: 6] and with RS facing for next row.
Place marker at beg of last row to denote top of side seam.
Work 18 [24: 28: 32] rows, ending after chart row 24 [24: 6: 6] and with RS facing for next row.

Shape back neck
Place marker at end of last row to denote right back neck point.
Keeping patt correct, dec 1 st at neck edge of next 2 rows, then on foll alt row. 59 [61: 65: 67] sts.
Work 43 [43: 47: 47] rows, ending after chart row 7 [7: 25: 25] and with **WS** facing for next row.
Inc 1 st at neck edge of next and foll alt row, then on foll row, ending after chart row 11 [11: 29: 29] and with **WS** facing for next row.
Place marker at beg of last row to denote left back neck point.
★★Work 17 [23: 27: 31] rows, ending after chart row 28 [2: 24: 28] and with RS facing for next row.
Place marker at beg of last row to denote top of side seam.
Work 6 rows, ending after chart row 2 [8: 30: 2] and with RS facing for next row.
Dec 1 st at end (underarm edge) of next and 8 [5: 6: 4] foll 6th rows, then on 3 [6: 7: 9] foll 4th rows and at same time dec 1 st at beg (overarm edge) of 11th [15th: 5th: 11th] and 7 foll 8th rows. 42 [44: 46: 48] sts.
Work 3 rows, ending after chart row 2 and with RS facing for next row.
Cast off in patt.

FRONT (worked sideways, beg at left cuff)
Work as given for back to beg of back neck shaping.

Shape front neck
Place marker at end of last row to denote left front neck point.
Keeping patt correct, dec 1 st at neck edge of next 7 rows, then on foll 3 alt rows. 52 [54: 58: 60] sts.
Work 25 [25: 29: 29] rows, ending after chart row 30 [30: 16: 16] and with RS facing for next row.
Inc 1 st at neck edge of next and foll 3 alt rows, then on foll 6 rows, ending after chart row 11 [11: 29: 29] and with **WS** facing for next row.
Place marker at end of last row to denote right front neck point.
Complete as given for back from ★★.

MAKING UP

Press as described on the information page.

Join both overarm and shoulder seams using back stitch, or mattress stitch if preferred.

Right cuff

With RS facing and using 6mm (US 10) needles, pick up and knit 41 [43: 45: 47] sts from cast-on edge of back, then 41 [43: 45: 47] sts from cast-off edge of front. 82 [86: 90: 94] sts.

Row 1 (WS): P1 [3: 1: 3], (P2tog) 40 [40: 44: 44] times, P1 [3: 1: 3]. 42 [46: 46: 50] sts.

Row 2: K2, *P2, K2, rep from * to end.

Row 3: P2, *K2, P2, rep from * to end.

Last 2 rows form rib.

Cont in rib until cuff meas 9 [12: 8: 11] cm from pick-up row, ending with RS facing for next row.

Cast off in rib.

Left cuff

With RS facing and using 6mm (US 10) needles, pick up and knit 41 [43: 45: 47] sts from cast-on edge of front, then 41 [43: 45: 47] sts from cast-off edge of back. 82 [86: 90: 94] sts.

Complete as given for right cuff.

Join underarm and cuff seams, from markers denoting base of side seams to cast-off edges of cuffs.

Hem border

With RS facing and using 6mm (US 10) circular needle, pick up and knit 64 [72: 80: 88] sts across lower row-end edge of back (between markers/seams), then 64 [72: 80: 88] sts across lower row-end edge of front (between markers/seams). 128 [144: 160: 176] sts.

Round 1 (RS): *K2, P2, rep from * to end.

Rep this round until hem border meas 16 cm from pick-up round.

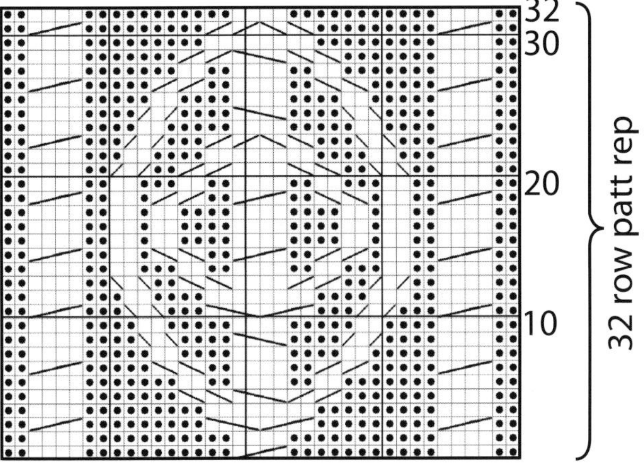

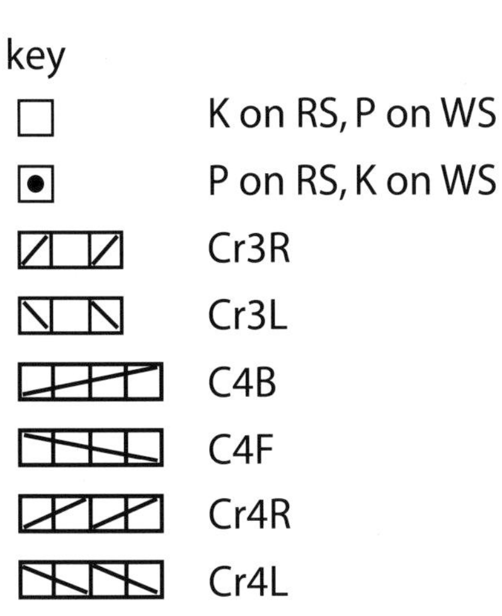

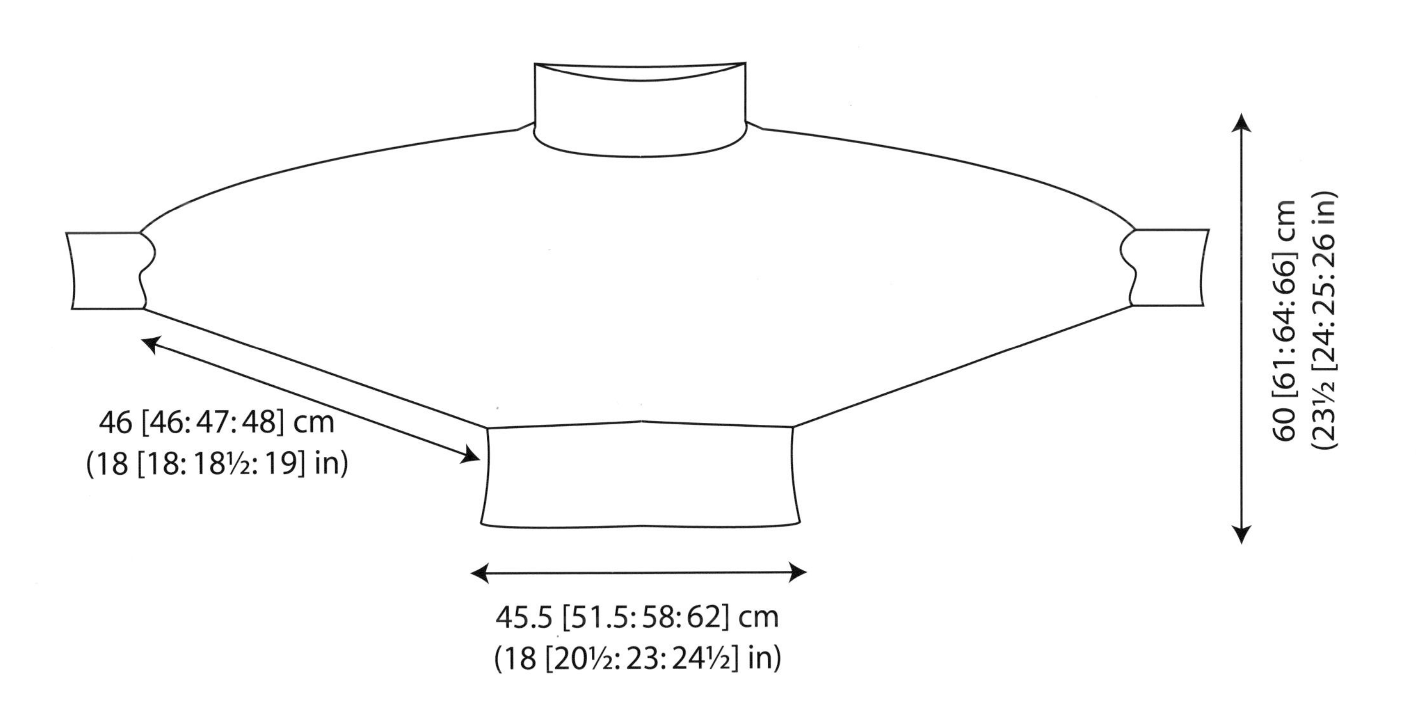

Cast off in rib.
Mark centre back and centre front neck points.
Collar
With RS facing and using 6mm (US 10) circular needle, beg and ending at centre back neck point, pick up and knit 26 [26: 28: 28] sts from left back neck edge to left shoulder seam, 30 [30: 32: 32] sts from left front neck edge to centre front neck point, 30 [30: 32: 32] sts from right front neck edge to right shoulder seam, then 26 [26: 28: 28] sts from right back neck edge to centre back neck point.
112 [112: 120: 120] sts.
Round 1 (RS): K1, P2, *K2, P2, rep from * to last st, K1.
This round forms rib.
Keeping rib correct, cont as folls:
Next row (RS): Rib 10, wrap next st (by slipping next st from left needle onto right needle, taking yarn to opposite side of work between needles and then slipping same st back onto left needle – when working back across wrapped sts work the wrapping loop and the wrapped st together) and turn.
Next row: Rib 20, wrap next st and turn.
Next row: Rib 30, wrap next st and turn.
Next row: Rib 40, wrap next st and turn.
Next row: Rib 50, wrap next st and turn.
Next row: Rib 60, wrap next st and turn.
Next row: Rib 70, wrap next st and turn.
Next row: Rib 80, wrap next st and turn.
Next row: Rib 40 (to return to centre back neck point).
Now work in **rounds** of rib until collar meas 9 cm **at centre front neck point.**
Cast off in rib.

YARN
Rowan Cocoon 6 x 100gm
(photographed in 812 Bilberry)

NEEDLES
1 pair of 7mm (no 2) (US 10½)needles
1 6mm (no 4) (US 10) crochet hook

TENSION
12 sts and 19 rows to 10cm measured over pattern using 7mm (US 10½) needles.

FINISHED SIZE
52cm x 190cm

UK CROCHET ABBREVIATIONS
ch = chain; **dc** = double crochet.

Selene Wrap
by Marie Wallin

Using 7mm (US 10½) needles and yarn A, cast on 62 sts.
Row 1 (RS): *K2, P2; rep from * to last 2 sts, K2.
Row 2: P2 *K2, P2; rep from * to end.
These 2 rows form 2 x 2 rib. Cont in rib for 6cm, ending with **WS** facing for next row.
Work grapevine pattern as follows:
Row 1 (WS): and all other WS rows – Purl.
Row 2: K2, *K2 tog, K1, yfwd, K1, Sl 1, K1, psso, K2; rep from *to last 4sts, K4.
Row 4: K1, K2 tog, K1, yfwd, *K1, yo, K1, Sl 1, K1, psso, K2 tog, K1, yfwd; rep from *to last 2sts, K2.
Row 6: K3, yfwd, *K3, yfwd, K1, Sl 1, K1, psso, K1, yfwd; rep from *to last 3sts, K3.
Row 8: K5, *K2 tog, K1, yfwd, K1, Sl 1, K1, psso, K2; rep from *to last 2sts, K2.
Row 10: K4, *K2 tog, K1, (yfwd, K1) twice, Sl 1, K1, psso; rep from *to last 3sts, K3.
Row 12: K3, K2 tog, *K1, yfwd, K3, yfwd, K1, K2 tog; rep from *to last 2sts, K2.
These 12 rows form the grapevine pattern. Continue in pattern until work measures 184cm from cast on edge, ending with **WS** facing for next row.
Next row (WS): Purl.
Work 6cm in 2 x 2 rib ending with RS facing for next row.
Cast off in rib.

EDGING
Using 6mm (US 10) crochet hook and with RS facing, join yarn at corner edge.
Next row: 1ch, dc evenly along row end edge, turn.
Next row: 1ch, 1dc in each dc to end.
Fasten off.
Work second row end edge in same way.

MAKING UP
Press as described on the information page.

SIZE	S	M	L	XL	XXL	
To fit bust	81-86	91-97	102-107	112-117	122-127	cm
	32-34	36-38	40-42	44-46	48-50	in

YARN

Rowan Cocoon	7	7	8	9	10	x 100gm

(photographed in Quarry Tile 818)

NEEDLES
1 pair 6mm (no 4) (US 10) needles, 1 pair 7mm (no 2) (US 10½) needles,
6mm (no 4) (US 10) circular needle & Cable needle

BUTTONS – 2 x 00422

TENSION
14 sts and 16 rows to 10 cm measured over st st using 7mm (US 10½) needles.

SPECIAL ABBREVIATIONS
C6B = slip next 3 sts onto cable needle and leave at back of work, K3, then K3 from cable needle;
C6F = slip next 3 sts onto cable needle and leave at front of work, K3, then K3 from cable needle.

BACK
Using 6mm (US 10) needles cast on 64 [70: 78: 88: 98] sts.
Row 1 (RS): Purl.
Row 2: Knit.
Change to 7mm (US 10½) needles.
Row 3: K5 [8: 12: 17: 22], ★(M1, K3, M1, K2) twice, M1, K2, M1, (K2, M1, K3, M1) twice★, K10, rep from ★ to ★ once more, K to end. 84 [90: 98: 108: 118] sts.
Row 4: P4 [7: 11: 16: 21], ★K2, P6, K2, P14, K2, P6, K2★, P8, rep from ★ to ★ once more, P to end.
Beg and ending rows as indicated and repeating the 24 row patt rep throughout, now work in patt from chart as folls:
Cont straight until back meas 33 [34: 35: 36: 37] cm, ending with RS facing for next row.
Shape armholes
Keeping patt correct, cast off 3 sts at beg of next 2 rows.
78 [84: 92: 102: 112] sts.
Dec 1 st at each end of next 5 [5: 7: 7: 9] rows, then on foll 2 [3: 3: 5: 5] alt rows. 64 [68: 72: 78: 84] sts.
Cont straight until armhole meas 19 [20: 21: 22: 23] cm, ending with RS facing for next row.
Shape shoulders and back neck
Next row (RS): Cast off 8 [9: 9: 10: 11] sts, patt until there are 11 [12: 12: 14: 15] sts on right needle and turn, leaving rem sts on a holder.
Work each side of neck separately.
Cast off 3 sts at beg of next row.
Cast off rem 8 [9: 9: 11: 12] sts.
With RS facing, rejoin yarn to rem sts, cast off centre 26 [26: 30: 30: 32] sts, patt to end.
Complete to match first side, reversing shapings.

LEFT FRONT
Using 6mm (US 10) needles cast on 28 [31: 35: 40: 45] sts.
Row 1 (RS): Purl.
Row 2: Knit.
Change to 7mm (US 10½) needles.
Row 3: K5 [8: 12: 17: 22], (M1, K3, M1, K2) twice, M1, K2, M1, (K2, M1, K3, M1) twice, K1. 38 [41: 45: 50: 55] sts.
Row 4: K2, P6, K2, P14, K2, P6, K2, P to end.
Beg and ending rows as indicated, now work in patt from chart as folls:
Cont straight until 12 rows less have been worked than on back to beg of armhole shaping, ending with RS facing for next row.

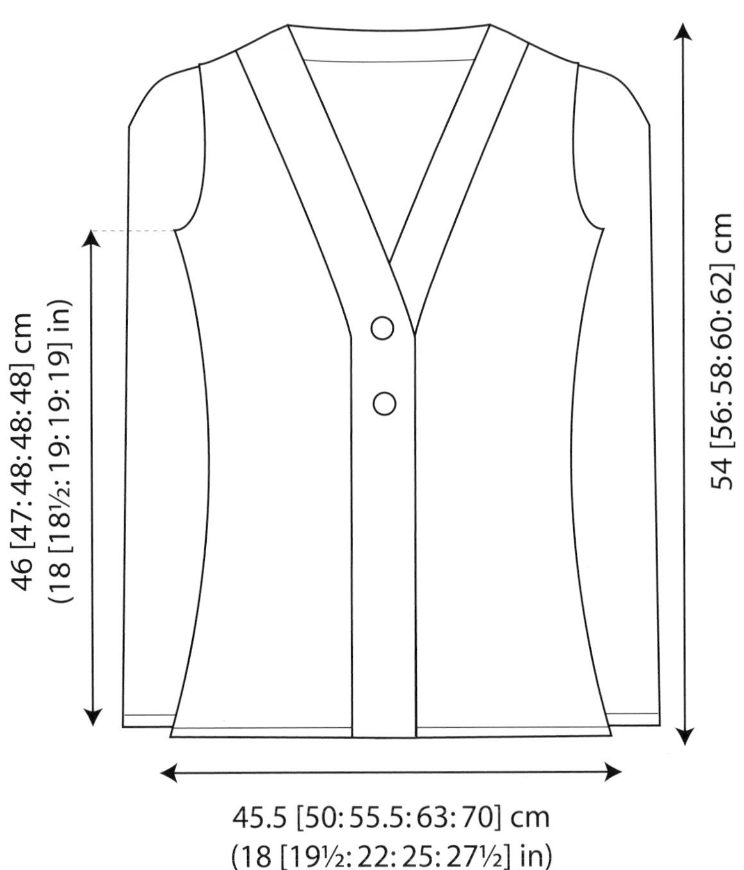

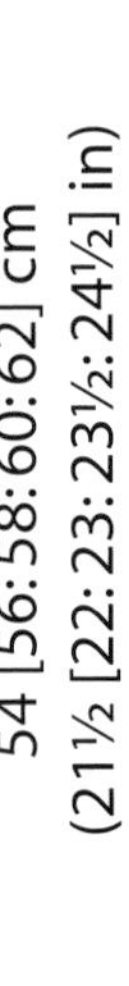

Shape front slope
Keeping patt correct, dec 1 st at end of next and foll 4 [3: 5: 5: 5] alt rows, then on 0 [1: 0: 0: 0] foll 4th row. 33 [36: 39: 44: 49] sts.
Work 3 [1: 1: 1: 1] rows, ending with RS facing for next row.
Shape armhole
Keeping patt correct, cast off 3 sts at beg and dec 1 [0: 1: 0: 1] st at end of next row. 29 [33: 35: 41: 45] sts.
Work 1 row.
Dec 1 st at armhole edge of next 5 [5: 7: 7: 9] rows, then on foll 2 [3: 3: 5: 5] alt rows **and at same time** dec 1 st at front slope edge of 3rd [next: 3rd: next: next] and 1 [2: 2: 4: 4] foll 4th rows.
20 [22: 22: 24: 26] sts.
Dec 1 st at front slope edge **only** on 2nd [2nd: 2nd: 4th: 2nd] and 3 [3: 3: 2: 2] foll 4th rows. 16 [18: 18: 21: 23] sts.
Cont straight until left front matches back to beg of shoulder shaping, ending with RS facing for next row.
Shape shoulder
Cast off 8 [9: 9: 10: 11] sts at beg of next row.
Work 1 row.
Cast off rem 8 [9: 9: 11: 12] sts.

RIGHT FRONT
Using 6mm (US 10) needles cast on 28 [31: 35: 40: 45] sts.
Row 1 (RS): Purl.
Row 2: Knit.
Change to 7mm (US 10½) needles.
Row 3: K1, (M1, K3, M1, K2) twice, M1, K2, M1, (K2, M1, K3, M1) twice, K to end. 38 [41: 45: 50: 55] sts.
Row 4: P4 [7: 11: 16: 21], K2, P6, K2, P14, K2, P6, K2.
Complete to match left front, reversing shapings.

SLEEVES
Using 6mm (US 10) needles cast on 31 [33: 33: 33: 35] sts.
Row 1 (RS): Purl.
Row 2: Knit.
Change to 7mm (US 10½) needles.
Beg with a K row, work in st st, shaping sides by inc 1 st at each end of 5th and every foll 6th row to 39 [39: 47: 55: 57] sts, then on every foll 8th [8th: 8th: -: -] row until there are 49 [51: 53: -: -] sts.
Cont straight until sleeve meas 46 [47: 48: 48: 48] cm, ending with RS facing for next row.
Shape top
Cast off 3 sts at beg of next 2 rows. 43 [45: 47: 49: 51] sts.
Dec 1 st at each end of next 3 rows, then on every foll alt row until 29 sts rem, then on foll 7 rows, ending with RS facing for next row.
Cast off rem 15 sts.

MAKING UP
Press as described on the information page.
Join both shoulder seams using back stitch, or mattress stitch if preferred.
Front band
With RS facing and using 6mm (US 10) circular needle, beg and ending at cast-on edges, pick up and knit 40 [42: 43: 45: 46] sts up right front opening edge to beg of front slope shaping, 41 [43: 43: 45: 47] sts up right front slope, 26 [26: 28: 28: 30] sts from back, 41 [43: 43: 45: 47] sts down left front slope to beg of front slope shaping, then 40 [42: 43: 45: 46] sts down left front opening edge. 188 [196: 200: 208: 216] sts.
Row 1 (WS): K1, P2, *K2, P2, rep from * to last st, K1.
Row 2: K3, *P2, K2, rep from * to last st, K1.
These 2 rows form rib.
Work in rib for 1 row more, ending with RS facing for next row.
Row 4 (RS): Rib 23 [25: 26: 28: 29], cast off 2 sts (to make first buttonhole), rib until there are 12 sts on right needle after cast-off, cast off 2 sts (to make 2nd buttonhole), rib to end.
Row 5: Rib to end, casting on 2 sts over those cast off on previous row.
Work in rib for a further 4 rows, ending with RS facing for next row.
Cast off in rib.
See information page for finishing instructions, setting in sleeves using the set-in method.

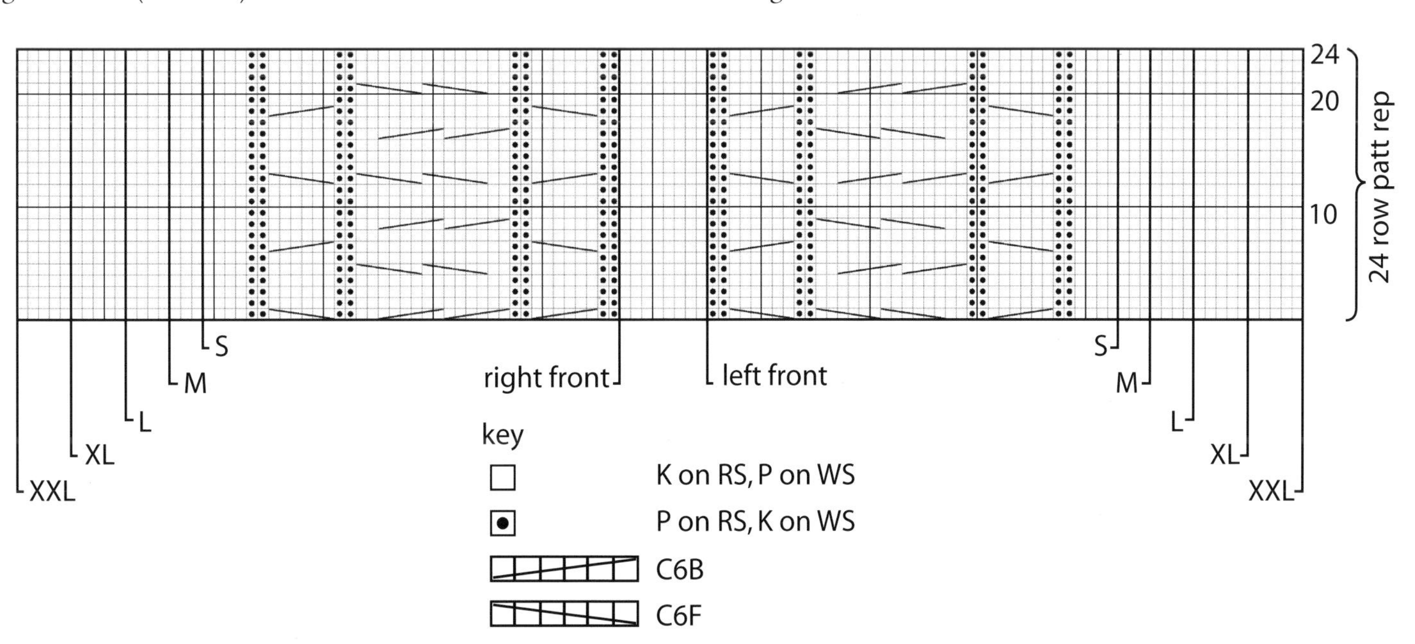

SIZE

	S	M	L	XL	XXL	
To fit bust						
	81-86	91-97	102-107	112-117	122-127	cm
	32-34	36-38	40-42	44-46	48-50	in

YARN
Rowan Cocoon

5	6	6	7	8	x 100gm

(photographed in Red Wine 819)

NEEDLES
1 pair 6mm (no 4) (US 10) needles
1 pair 7mm (no 2) (US 10½) needles

BUTTONS – 1 x 00422

TENSION
14 sts and 16 rows to 10 cm measured over st st using 7mm (US 10½) needles.

BACK
Using 6mm (US 10) needles cast on 63 [71: 79: 87: 97] sts.
Row 1 (RS): P1, *K1, P1, rep from * to end.
Row 2: As row 1.
These 2 rows form moss st.
Work in moss st for a further 20 rows, ending with RS facing for next row.
Change to 7mm (US 10½) needles.
Beg with a K row, work in st st for 26 [28: 28: 30: 32] rows, ending with RS facing for next row. (Back should meas 25 [26: 27: 28: 29] cm.)
Shape armholes
Cast off 3 sts at beg of next 2 rows. 57 [65: 73: 81: 91] sts.
Dec 1 st at each end of next 3 [5: 5: 7: 9] rows, then on foll 1 [2: 3: 3: 4] alt rows. 49 [51: 57: 61: 65] sts.
Cont straight until armhole meas 19 [20: 21: 22: 23] cm, ending with RS facing for next row.
Shape shoulders and back neck
Next row (RS): Cast off 5 [6: 7: 8: 9] sts, K until there are 9 [9: 10: 11: 12] sts on right needle and turn, leaving rem sts on a holder.
Work each side of neck separately.
Cast off 3 sts at beg of next row.
Cast off rem 6 [6: 7: 8: 9] sts.
With RS facing, rejoin yarn to rem sts, cast off centre 21 [21: 23: 23: 23] sts, K to end.
Complete to match first side, reversing shapings.

LEFT FRONT
Using 6mm (US 10) needles cast on 36 [40: 44: 48: 53] sts.
Row 1 (RS): *P1, K1, rep from * to last 10 [10: 10: 10: 9] sts, P1 [1: 1: 1: 0], K9.
Row 2: K9, P1 [1: 1: 1: 0], *K1, P1, rep from * to end.
These 2 rows set the sts – front opening edge 9 sts in g st with all other sts in moss st.
Cont as set for a further 19 rows, ending with **WS** facing for next row.
Row 22 (WS): K9 and slip these sts onto a holder, moss st to end. 27 [31: 35: 39: 44] sts.
Change to 7mm (US 10½) needles.
Beg with a K row, work in st st for 4 rows, ending with RS facing for next row.
Shape front slope
Dec 1 st at end of next and 1 [0: 1: 0: 0] foll 4th row, then on 2 [3: 3: 4: 4] foll 6th rows. 23 [27: 30: 34: 39] sts.
Work 5 [5: 1: 1: 3] rows, ending with RS facing.
Shape armhole
Cast off 3 sts at beg and dec 1 [1: 0: 0: 0] st at end of next row. 19 [23: 27: 31: 36] sts.
Work 1 row.
Dec 1 st at armhole edge of next 3 [5: 5: 7: 9] rows, then on foll 1 [2: 3: 3: 4] alt rows **and at same time** dec 1 st at front slope edge of 5th [5th: 3rd: 3rd: next] and 0 [0: 1: 1: 2] foll 6th rows.
14 [15: 17: 19: 20] sts.
Dec 1 st at front slope edge **only** on 6th [2nd: 4th: 2nd: 4th] and 2 [1: 2: 2: 0] foll 6th rows, then on 0 [1: 0: 0: 1] foll 8th row.
11 [12: 14: 16: 18] sts.
Cont straight until left front matches back to beg of shoulder shaping, ending with RS facing for next row.
Shape shoulder
Cast off 5 [6: 7: 8: 9] sts at beg of next row.
Work 1 row.
Cast off rem 6 [6: 7: 8: 9] sts.

RIGHT FRONT
Using 6mm (US 10) needles cast on 36 [40: 44: 48: 53] sts.
Row 1 (RS): K9, P1 [1: 1: 1: 0], *K1, P1, rep from * to end.
Row 2: *P1, K1, rep from * to last 10 [10: 10: 10: 9] sts, P1 [1: 1: 1: 0], K9.
These 2 rows set the sts – front opening edge 9 sts in g st with all other sts in moss st.
Cont as set for a further 19 rows, ending with **WS** facing for next row.

Row 22 (WS): Moss st to last 9 sts and turn, leaving rem 9 sts on a holder. 27 [31: 35: 39: 44] sts.
Complete to match left front, reversing shapings.

SLEEVES
Using 6mm (US 10) needles cast on 31 [33: 33: 33: 35] sts.
Work in moss st as given for back for 16 rows, ending with RS facing for next row.
Change to 7mm (US 10½) needles.
Beg with a K row, work in st st, shaping sides by inc 1 st at each end of 3rd and every foll 4th row to 37 [37: 41: 47: 49] sts, then on every foll 6th row until there are 51 [53: 55: 57: 59] sts.
Cont straight until sleeve meas 46 [47: 48: 48: 48] cm, ending with RS facing for next row.
Shape top
Cast off 3 sts at beg of next 2 rows. 45 [47: 49: 51: 53] sts.
Dec 1 st at each end of next 3 rows, then on every foll alt row until 29 sts rem, then on foll 7 rows, ending with RS facing for next row.
Cast off rem 15 sts.

MAKING UP
Press as described on the information page.
Join both shoulder seams using back stitch, or mattress stitch if preferred.
Left front band
Slip 9 sts on left front holder onto 6mm (US 10) needles and rejoin yarn with RS facing.
Cont in g st until left front band, when slightly stretched, fits up left front slope and across to centre back neck, ending with RS facing for next row.
Cast off.
Right front band
Slip 9 sts on right front holder onto 6mm (US 10) needles and rejoin yarn with **WS** facing.
Next row (WS): K9.
Next row: K4, cast off 2 sts (to make a buttonhole – cast on 2 sts over these cast-off sts on next row), K to end.
Cont in g st until right front band, when slightly stretched, fits up right front slope and across to centre back neck, ending with RS facing for next row.
Cast off.
Join cast-off edges of bands, then neatly slip stitch bands in place.
See information page for finishing instructions, setting in sleeves using the set-in method.

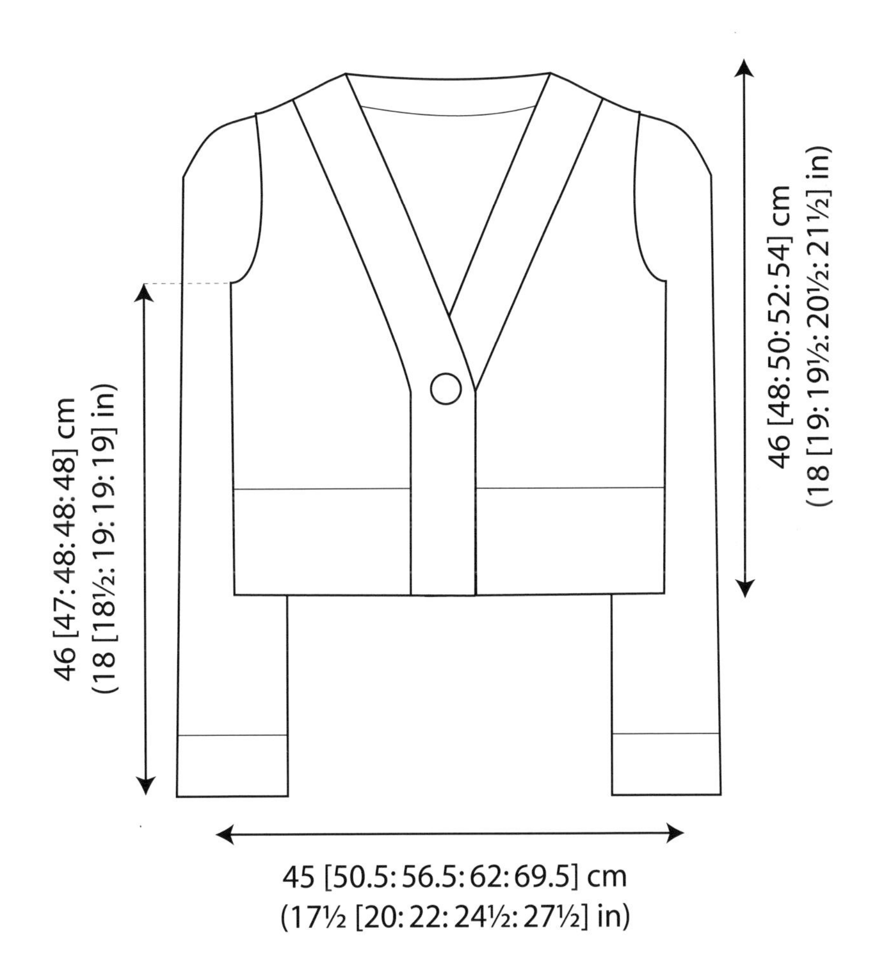

SIZE	S	M	L	XL	XXL	
To fit bust	81-86	91-97	102-107	112-117	122-127	cm
	32-34	36-38	40-42	44-46	48-50	in
YARN						
Rowan Cocoon	7	8	9	9	10	x 100gm

(photographed in Bilberry 812)

NEEDLES
1 pair 6mm (no 4) (US 10) needles, 1 pair 7mm (no 2) (US 10½) needles &
5.00mm (no 6) (US H8) crochet hook

TENSION
14 sts and 20 rows to 10 cm measured over pattern using 7mm (US 10½) needles.

SPECIAL ABBREVIATIONS
MB = (K1, P1, K1, P1, K1) all into next st, lift 2nd, 3rd, 4th and 5th sts on right needle over first st and off needle.

UK CROCHET ABBREVIATIONS
ch = chain; **dc** = double crochet.

BACK
Using 6mm (US 10) needles cast on 66 [70: 78: 90: 98] sts.
Row 1 (RS): K2, *P2, K2, rep from * to end.
Row 2: P2, *K2, P2, rep from * to end.
These 2 rows form rib.
Work in rib for a further 4 rows, dec [inc: inc: dec: inc] 1 st at end of last row and ending with RS facing for next row. 65 [71: 79: 89: 99] sts.
Change to 7mm (US 10½) needles.
Cont in patt as folls:
Row 1 (RS): K3 [4: 5: 6: 7], work next 15 sts as row 1 of patt panel, K29 [33: 39: 47: 55], work next 15 sts as row 1 of patt panel, K3 [4: 5: 6: 7].
Row 2: P3 [4: 5: 6: 7], work next 15 sts as row 2 of patt panel, P29 [33: 39: 47: 55], work next 15 sts as row 2 of patt panel, P3 [4: 5: 6: 7].
These 2 rows set the sts – 2 patt panels with st st at sides and centre.
Cont as now set for a further 42 rows, ending after patt panel row 2 and with RS facing for next row.
Next row (waist eyelet row) (RS): K2 [5: 5: 2: 3], yfwd, K2tog, *K2, yfwd, K2tog, rep from * to last 1 [4: 4: 1: 2] sts, K1 [4: 4: 1: 2].
Next row: Purl.
Now cont in patt as folls:
Row 1 (RS): K3 [4: 5: 6: 7], work next 15 sts as row 1 of patt panel, K29 [33: 39: 47: 55], work next 15 sts as row 1 of patt panel, K3 [4: 5: 6: 7].
Row 2: P3 [4: 5: 6: 7], work next 15 sts as row 2 of patt panel, P29 [33: 39: 47: 55], work next 15 sts as row 2 of patt panel, P3 [4: 5: 6: 7].
These 2 rows set the sts – 2 patt panels with st st at sides and centre.
Cont as set until back meas 39 cm, ending with RS facing for next row.
Shape for sleeves
Inc 1 st at each end of next and foll alt row, then on foll 3 rows, taking inc sts into st st and ending with RS facing for next row.
75 [81: 89: 99: 109] sts.
Next row (RS): Cast on 19 sts, work across these 19 sts as folls: K3, P2, K2, P2, K10, patt to end.
Next row: Cast on 19 sts, work across these 19 sts as folls: K1, (P2, K2) twice, P10, patt to last 19 sts, P10, (K2, P2) twice, K1.
113 [119: 127: 137: 147] sts.
Place markers at both ends of last row.
Working same patt panel row on sleeve sts as on main sts, cont as folls:
Next row (RS): K3, P2, K2, P2, work next 15 sts as patt panel, K3 [4: 5: 6: 7], work next 15 sts as patt panel, K29 [33: 39: 47: 55], work next 15 sts as patt panel, K3 [4: 5: 6: 7], work next 15 sts as patt panel, P2, K2, P2, K3.
Next row: K1, (P2, K2) twice, work next 15 sts as patt panel, P3 [4: 5: 6: 7], work next 15 sts as patt panel, P29 [33: 39: 47: 55], work next 15 sts as patt panel, P3 [4: 5: 6: 7], work next 15 sts as patt panel, (K2, P2) twice, K1.
These 2 rows set the sts – 4 patt panels with st st between, and first and last 9 sts of every row now in rib.
Cont as set until armhole meas 24 [25: 26: 27: 28] cm from markers, ending with RS facing for next row.
Shape shoulders and back neck
Next row (RS): Cast off 22 [23: 25: 27: 29] sts, patt until there are 25 [27: 28: 31: 33] sts on right needle and turn, leaving rem sts on a holder.
Work each side of neck separately.
Cast off 3 sts at beg of next row.
Cast off rem 22 [24: 25: 28: 30] sts.
With RS facing, rejoin yarn to rem sts, cast off centre 19 [19: 21: 21: 23] sts, patt to end.
Complete to match first side, reversing shapings.

LEFT FRONT
Using 6mm (US 10) needles cast on 31 [35: 39: 43: 47] sts.
Row 1 (RS): K2, *P2, K2, rep from * to last st, K1.
Row 2: K1, P2, *K2, P2, rep from * to end.
These 2 rows form rib.

Work in rib for a further 4 rows, dec 1 [2: 2: 1: 0] sts evenly across last row and ending with RS facing for next row.
30 [33: 37: 42: 47] sts.
Change to 7mm (US 10½) needles.
Cont in patt as folls:
Row 1 (RS): K3 [4: 5: 6: 7], work next 15 sts as row 1 of patt panel, K12 [14: 17: 21: 25].
Row 2: P12 [14: 17: 21: 25], work next 15 sts as row 2 of patt panel, P3 [4: 5: 6: 7].
These 2 rows set the sts – patt panel with st st at either side.
Cont as now set for a further 42 rows, ending after patt panel row 2 and with RS facing for next row.
Next row (waist eyelet row) (RS): K2 [5: 5: 2: 3], *yfwd, K2tog, K2, rep from * to end.
Next row: Purl.
Now cont in patt as folls:
Row 1 (RS): K3 [4: 5: 6: 7], work next 15 sts as row 1 of patt panel, K12 [14: 17: 21: 25].
Row 2: P12 [14: 17: 21: 25], work next 15 sts as row 2 of patt panel, P3 [4: 5: 6: 7].
These 2 rows set the sts – patt panel with st st at either side.
Cont as set until left front meas 39 cm, ending with RS facing for next row.

Shape for sleeve

Inc 1 st at beg of next and foll alt row, then at same edge on foll 3 rows, taking inc sts into st st and ending with RS facing for next row. 35 [38: 42: 47: 52] sts.
Next row (RS): Cast on 19 sts, work across these 19 sts as folls: K3, P2, K2, P2, K10, patt to end. 54 [57: 61: 66: 71] sts.
Next row: Patt to last 19 sts, P10, (K2, P2) twice, K1.
Place marker at end of last row.

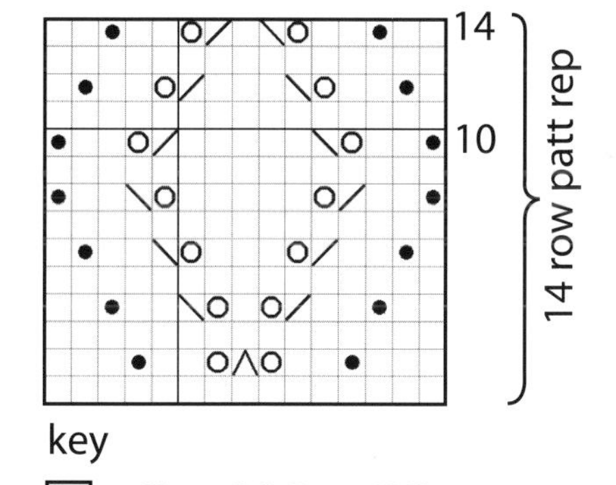

key

- K on RS, P on WS
- MB
- yrn
- P2tog
- P2tog tbl
- slip 2sts, P1, pass 2 slipped sts over

Working same patt panel row on sleeve sts as on main sts, cont as folls:
Next row (RS): K3, P2, K2, P2, work next 15 sts as patt panel, K3 [4: 5: 6: 7], work next 15 sts as patt panel, K12 [14: 17: 21: 25].
Next row: P12 [14: 17: 21: 25], work next 15 sts as patt panel, P3 [4: 5: 6: 7], work next 15 sts as patt panel, (K2, P2) twice, K1.
These 2 rows set the sts – 2 patt panels with st st between and at centre front, and armhole edge 9 sts now in rib.
Cont as set until 1 row less has been worked than on back to beg of shoulder shaping, ending with **WS** facing for next row.

Shape front neck and shoulder

Cast off 5 [5: 5: 5: 6] sts at beg of next row, 22 [23: 25: 27: 29] sts at beg of foll row, then 5 [5: 6: 6: 6] sts at beg of next row.
Cast off rem 22 [24: 25: 28: 30] sts.

RIGHT FRONT

Using 6mm (US 10) needles cast on 31 [35: 39: 43: 47] sts.
Row 1 (RS): K3, *P2, K2, rep from * to end.
Row 2: P2, *K2, P2, rep from * to last st, K1.
These 2 rows form rib.
Work in rib for a further 4 rows, dec 1 [2: 2: 1: 0] sts evenly across last row and ending with RS facing for next row.
30 [33: 37: 42: 47] sts.
Change to 7mm (US 10½) needles.
Cont in patt as folls:
Row 1 (RS): K12 [14: 17: 21: 25], work next 15 sts as row 1 of patt panel, K3 [4: 5: 6: 7].
Row 2: P3 [4: 5: 6: 7], work next 15 sts as row 2 of patt panel, P12 [14: 17: 21: 25].
These 2 rows set the sts – patt panel with st st at either side.
Cont as now set for a further 42 rows, ending after patt panel row 2 and with RS facing for next row.
Next row (waist eyelet row) (RS): K3, yfwd, K2tog, *K2, yfwd, K2tog, rep from * to last 1 [4: 4: 1: 2] sts, K1 [4: 4: 1: 2].
Next row: Purl.
Now cont in patt as folls:
Row 1 (RS): K12 [14: 17: 21: 25], work next 15 sts as row 1 of patt panel, K3 [4: 5: 6: 7].
Row 2: P3 [4: 5: 6: 7], work next 15 sts as row 2 of patt panel, P12 [14: 17: 21: 25].
These 2 rows set the sts – patt panel with st st at either side.
Cont as set until right front meas 39 cm, ending with RS facing for next row.

Shape for sleeve

Inc 1 st at end of next and foll alt row, then at same edge on foll 3 rows, taking inc sts into st st and ending with RS facing for next row. 35 [38: 42: 47: 52] sts.
Work 1 row.
Next row (WS): Cast on 19 sts, work across these 19 sts as folls: K1, (P2, K2) twice, P10, patt to end. 54 [57: 61: 66: 71] sts.
Place marker at beg of last row.
Working same patt panel row on sleeve sts as on main sts, cont as folls:
Next row (RS): K12 [14: 17: 21: 25], work next 15 sts as patt

panel, K3 [4: 5: 6: 7], work next 15 sts as patt panel, P2, K2, P2, K3.
Next row: K1, (P2, K2) twice, work next 15 sts as patt panel, P3 [4: 5: 6: 7], work next 15 sts as patt panel, P12 [14: 17: 21: 25].
These 2 rows set the sts – 2 patt panels with st st between and at centre front, and armhole edge 9 sts now in rib.
Complete to match left front, reversing shapings.

MAKING UP
Press as described on the information page.
Join both shoulder/overarm seams using back stitch, or mattress stitch if preferred.
Front bands (both alike)
With RS facing and using 6mm (US 10) needles, pick up and knit 98 [102: 102: 106: 106] sts evenly along front opening edge, between cast-on edge and top of neck band.
Beg with row 2, work in rib as given for back for 1 row, ending with RS facing for next row.
Place marker on st level with waist eyelet row.
Row 2 (RS): Rib to marked st, yrn, work 2 tog (to make eyelet hole), rib to end.
Work in rib for 3 rows.
Rep last 4 rows 3 times more, then the first of these rows (the eyelet row) again.
Work a further 2 rows.
Cast off in rib.
Neckband
With **WS** facing and using 6mm (US 10) needles, pick up and knit 14 sts along upper row-end edge of left front band.
Break yarn and leave sts on a holder.
With **WS** facing and using 6mm (US 10) needles, pick up and knit 14 sts along upper row-end edge of right front band.
Break yarn and leave sts on a holder.
With **RS** facing and using 6mm (US 10) needles, beg and ending at front band pick-up rows, pick up and knit 10 [10: 11: 11: 12] sts up right side of neck, 26 [26: 28: 28: 30] sts from back, then 10 [10: 11: 11: 12] sts down left side of neck. 46 [46: 50: 50: 54] sts.
Break yarn and leave sts on a holder.
With **WS** facing and using 6mm (US 10) needles, work across all 3 sets of sts as folls: K2, (P2, K2) 3 times across 14 sts at top of left front band, P2, (K2, P2) 11 [11: 12: 12: 13] times across centre set of sts, then K2, (P2, K2) 3 times across 14 sts at top of right front band. 74 [74: 78: 78: 82] sts.
Work in rib as set for 1 row more.
Cast off in rib.
Fold front bands back onto fronts, folding band so that first and 2nd eyelets match each other and rem 3 eyelets match first 3 waist eyelets of front. (4 eyelets should be visible on RS of front band.)
Tie
Using 5.00mm (US H8) crochet hook, make a ch 150 [160: 170: 180: 190] cm long.
Row 1: 1 dc into 2nd ch from hook, 1 dc into each ch to end.
Fasten off.
See information page for finishing instructions. Using photograph as a guide, thread tie through waist eyelet row.

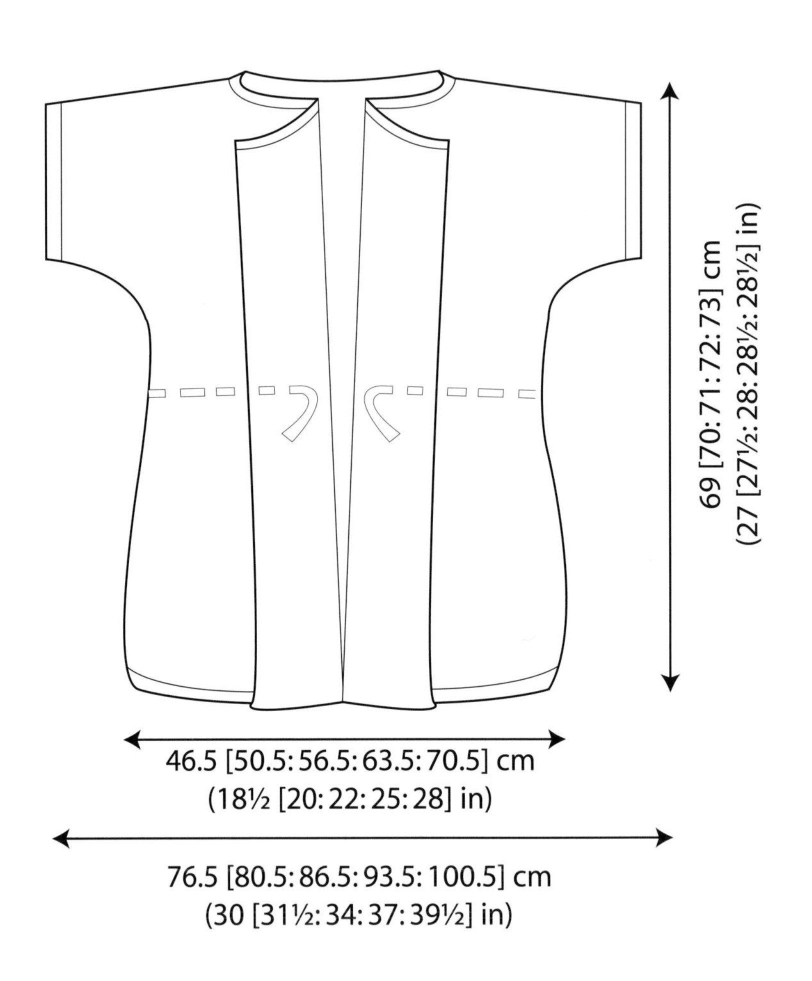

SIZE	S	M	L	XL	XXL	
To fit bust	81-86	91-97	102-107	112-117	122-127	cm
	32-34	36-38	40-42	44-46	48-50	in
YARN						
Rowan Cocoon	8	9	10	10	11	x 100gm
(photographed in Scree 803)						

NEEDLES
1 pair 6mm (no 4) (US 10) needles, 1 pair 7mm (no 2) (US 10½) needles, 6.00mm (no 4) (US J10) crochet hook & Cable needle

BUTTONS – 2 x 00421

TENSION
14 sts and 16 rows to 10 cm measured over rev st st using 7mm (US 10½) needles. Cable panel A meas 19 cm.

UK CROCHET ABBREVIATIONS
ch = chain; **ss** = slip stitch; **dc** = double crochet; **sp** = space.

SPECIAL ABBREVIATIONS
Cr3R = slip next st onto cable needle and leave at back of work, K2, then P1 from cable needle;
Cr3L = slip next 2 sts onto cable needle and leave at front of work, P1, then K2 from cable needle;
C4B = slip next 2 sts onto cable needle and leave at back of work, K2, then K2 from cable needle;
C4F = slip next 2 sts onto cable needle and leave at front of work, K2, then K2 from cable needle;
C9F = slip next 5 sts onto cable needle and leave at front of work, K4, slip the P st back onto left needle and P this st, then K4 from cable needle;
C12B = slip next 8 sts onto cable needle and leave at back of work, K4, slip centre 4 sts (of original 12 sts) back onto left needle and K these 4 sts, then K4 from cable needle;
C12F = slip next 8 sts onto cable needle and leave at front of work, K4, slip centre 4 sts (of original 12 sts) back onto left needle and K these 4 sts, then K4 from cable needle.

CABLE PANEL A (37 sts)
Note: Number of sts varies whilst working cable panel. All st counts given throughout garment instructions presume there are 37 sts in cable panel A at all times. When working shaping through this panel, adjust the number of sts cast-off or decreased to cater for any extra sts in cable panel.
Row 1 (RS): (P2, K4) 3 times, P1, (K4, P2) 3 times.
Row 2: (K2, P4) 3 times, K1, (P4, K2) 3 times.
Row 3: P2, K4, P2, C4F, P2, K4, P1, K4, P2, C4B, P2, K4, P2.
Row 4: As row 2.
Rows 5 and 6: As rows 1 and 2.
Row 7: P2, K4, P2, C4F, P2, C9F, P2, C4B, P2, K4, P2.
Row 8: As row 2.
Row 9: P2, *M1, (K4, P2) twice, K4, M1*, P1, rep from * to * once more, P2. 41 sts.
Row 10: *K3, P4, (K2, P4) twice, rep from * once more, K3.
Row 11: P3, M1, K4, P2tog, C4F, P2tog, K4, M1, P3, M1, K4, P2tog, C4B, P2tog, K4, M1, P3. 41 sts.
Row 12: K4, *(P4, K1) twice, P4*, K5, rep from * to * once more, K4.
Row 13: P4, *M1, K3, sl 1, K1, psso, K4, K2tog, K3, M1*, P5, rep from * to * once more, P4.
Row 14: K5, P12, K7, P12, K5.
Row 15: P5, M1, K4, C4F, K4, M1, P7, M1, K4, C4B, K4, M1, P5. 45 sts.
Row 16: K6, P12, K9, P12, K6.
Row 17: P6, C12B, P9, C12F, P6.
Row 18: As row 16.
Row 19: P4, P2tog, K4, C4F, K4, P2tog, P5, P2tog, K4, C4B, K4, P2tog, P4. 41 sts.
Row 20: As row 14.
Row 21: P3, *P2tog, (K4, M1) twice, K4, P2tog, P3, rep from * once more. 41 sts.
Row 22: As row 12.
Row 23: P2, P2tog, K4, M1, P1, C4F, P1, M1, K4, P2tog, P1, P2tog, K4, M1, P1, C4B, P1, M1, K4, P2tog, P2. 41 sts.
Row 24: As row 10.
Row 25: P1, P2tog, *(K4, P2) twice, K4*, P3tog, rep from * to * once more, P2tog, P1. 37 sts.
Row 26: As row 2.
Row 27: As row 7.
Row 28: As row 2.
These 28 rows form cable panel A and are repeated.

BACK
Using 6mm (US 10) needles cast on 66 [74: 82: 90: 100] sts.
Work in g st for 3 rows, ending with **WS** facing for next row.
Row 4 (WS): K6 [10: 14: 18: 23], M1, (K3, M1) 8 times, K2, M1, K2, M1, K2, (M1, K3) 8 times, M1, K6 [10: 14: 18: 23].
86 [94: 102: 110: 120] sts.
Change to 7mm (US 10½) needles.
Now work in patt as folls:
Row 1 (RS): P4 [8: 12: 16: 21], work next 37 sts as row 1 of cable

panel A, C4B, work next 37 sts as row 1 of cable panel A, P to end.
Row 2: K4 [8: 12: 16: 21], work next 37 sts as row 2 of cable panel A, P4, work next 37 sts as row 2 of cable panel A, K to end.
Row 3: P4 [8: 12: 16: 21], work next 37 sts as row 3 of cable panel A, K4, work next 37 sts as row 3 of cable panel A, P to end.
Row 4: K4 [8: 12: 16: 21], work next 37 sts as row 4 of cable panel A, P4, work next 37 sts as row 4 of cable panel A, K to end.
These 4 rows set the sts – 2 reps of cable panel A with cable between and rev st st at sides.
Keeping sts correct throughout as now set, cont straight until back meas 27 [28: 29: 30: 31] cm, ending with RS facing for next row.

Shape armholes

Keeping patt correct, cast off 2 sts at beg of next 2 rows.
82 [90: 98: 106: 116] sts.
Dec 1 st at each end of next 1 [3: 5: 7: 9] rows, then on foll 0 [1: 1: 1: 2] alt rows. 80 [82: 86: 90: 94] sts.
Cont straight until armhole meas 19 [20: 21: 22: 23] cm, ending with RS facing for next row.

Shape shoulders and back neck

Next row (RS): Cast off 11 [11: 12: 13: 14] sts, patt until there are 14 [15: 16: 17: 17] sts on right needle and turn, leaving rem sts on a holder.
Work each side of neck separately.
Cast off 3 sts at beg of next row.
Cast off rem 11 [12: 13: 14: 14] sts.
With RS facing, rejoin yarn to rem sts, cast off centre 30 [30: 30: 30: 32] sts, patt to end.
Complete to match first side, reversing shapings.

LEFT FRONT

Using 6mm (US 10) needles cast on 46 [50: 54: 58: 63] sts.
Work in g st for 3 rows, ending with **WS** facing for next row.
Row 4 (WS): Cast off 3 sts (one st on right needle), K2, M1, (K2, M1) twice, (K3, M1) 8 times, (K2, M1) twice, K8 [12: 16: 20: 25]. 56 [60: 64: 68: 73] sts.
Change to 7mm (US 10½) needles.
Now work in patt as folls:
Row 1 (RS): P8 [12: 16: 20: 25], C4B, work next 37 sts as row 1 of cable panel A, C4B, P3.
Row 2: K3, P4, work next 37 sts as row 2 of cable panel A, P4, K to end.
Row 3: P8 [12: 16: 20: 25], K4, work next 37 sts as row 3 of cable panel A, K4, P3.
Row 4: K3, P4, work next 37 sts as row 4 of cable panel A, P4, K to end.
These 4 rows set the sts – 1 rep of cable panel A with cables either side and rev st st at sides.
Keeping sts correct throughout as now set, cont straight until left front matches back to beg of armhole shaping, ending with RS facing for next row.

Shape armhole

Keeping patt correct, cast off 2 sts at beg of next row. 54 [58: 62: 66: 71] sts.
Work 1 row.
Dec 1 st at armhole edge of next 1 [3: 5: 7: 9] rows, then on foll 0 [1: 1: 1: 2] alt rows. 53 [54: 56: 58: 60] sts.
Cont straight until 11 [11: 13: 13: 15] rows less have been worked than on back to beg of shoulder shaping, ending with **WS** facing for next row.

Shape neck

Keeping patt correct, cast off 25 [25: 24: 24: 24] sts at beg of next row. 28 [29: 32: 34: 36] sts.
Dec 1 st at neck edge of next 5 rows, then on foll 1 [1: 2: 2: 3] alt rows. 22 [23: 25: 27: 28] sts.
Work 3 rows, ending with RS facing for next row.

Shape shoulder

Cast off 11 [11: 12: 13: 14] sts at beg of next row.
Work 1 row.
Cast off rem 11 [12: 13: 14: 14] sts.

RIGHT FRONT

Using 6mm (US 10) needles cast on 46 [50: 54: 58: 63] sts.
Work in g st for 3 rows, ending with **WS** facing for next row.
Row 4 (WS): K8 [12: 16: 20: 25], (M1, K2) twice, (M1, K3) 8 times, (M1, K2) twice, M1, K3, cast off rem 3 sts. 56 [60: 64: 68: 73] sts.
Change to 7mm (US 10½) needles.
Rejoin yarn with RS facing and now work in patt as folls:
Row 1 (RS): P3, C4B, work next 37 sts as row 1 of cable panel A, C4B, P to end.
Row 2: K8 [12: 16: 20: 25], P4, work next 37 sts as row 2 of cable panel A, P4, K to end.
Row 3: P3, K4, work next 37 sts as row 3 of cable panel A, K4, P to end.
Row 4: K8 [12: 16: 20: 25], P4, work next 37 sts as row 4 of cable panel A, P4, K to end.
These 4 rows set the sts – 1 rep of cable panel A with cables either side and rev st st at sides.
Complete to match left front, reversing shapings.

SLEEVES

Using 6mm (US 10) needles cast on 34 [36: 36: 36: 38] sts.
Work in g st for 3 rows, ending with **WS** facing for next row.
Row 4 (WS): K9 [10: 10: 10: 11], M1, K2, M1, K12, M1, K2, M1, K to end. 38 [40: 40: 40: 42] sts.
Change to 7mm (US 10½) needles.
Now work in patt as folls:
Row 1 (RS): P5 [6: 6: 6: 7], work next 12 sts as row 1 of cable

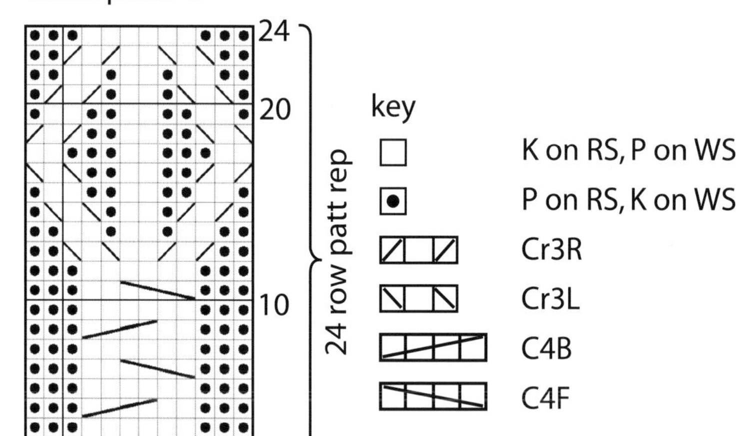

panel B, P4, work next 12 sts as row 1 of cable panel B, P to end.
Row 2: K5 [6: 6: 6: 7], work next 12 sts as row 2 of cable panel B, K4, work next 12 sts as row 2 of cable panel B, K to end.
These 2 rows set the sts – 2 reps of cable panel B with rev st st between and at sides.
Keeping sts correct throughout as now set, cont in patt, shaping sides by inc 1 st at each end of next and every foll 4th row to 44 [44: 48: 54: 56] sts, then on every foll 6th row until there are 60 [62: 64: 66: 68] sts, taking inc sts into rev st st.
Cont straight until sleeve meas 45 [46: 47: 47: 47] cm, ending with RS facing for next row.

Shape top

Keeping patt correct, cast off 2 sts at beg of next 2 rows.
56 [58: 60: 62: 64] sts.
Dec 1 st at each end of next 12 [12: 14: 14: 16] rows, ending with RS facing for next row. 32 [34: 32: 34: 32] sts.
Cast off 4 [5: 4: 5: 4] sts at beg of next 2 rows, then 5 sts at beg of foll 2 rows.
Cast off rem 14 sts.

MAKING UP

Press as described on the information page.
Join both shoulder seams using back stitch, or mattress stitch if preferred. (**Note**: Patt does **NOT** match across shoulder seams.)

Front bands (both alike)

With RS facing and using 6mm (US 10) needles, pick up and knit 53 [56: 57: 60: 62] sts along front opening edge, between top of cast-off sts near lower edge and neck edge.
Work in g st for 4 rows, ending with **WS** facing for next row.
Cast off knitwise (on **WS**).
Sew row-end edges of bands to cast-off sts near lower edge.

Neck edging and collar

With RS facing and using 6mm (US 10) needles, beg and ending at cast-off edges of front bands, pick up and knit 26 [26: 25: 25: 25] sts from right front neck edge, 11 [11: 13: 13: 15] sts up right front slope, 26 [26: 26: 26: 28] sts from back, 11 [11: 13: 13: 15] sts down left front slope, then 26 [26: 25: 25: 25] sts from left front neck edge. 100 [100: 102: 102: 108] sts.
Row 1 (WS): Cast off first 18 sts knitwise (one st on right needle), K2 [2: 0: 0: 6], inc in next st, (K2, inc in next st) 19 [19: 21: 21: 19] times, K3 [3: 1: 1: 7], cast off rem 18 sts knitwise.
With RS of body (WS of collar) facing, rejoin yarn to 84 [84: 88: 88: 92] sts and cont as folls:
Row 2: K1, P2, *K2, P2, rep from * to last st, K1.
Row 3: K3, *P2, K2, rep from * to last st, K1.
These 2 rows form rib.
Keeping rib correct, cont as folls:
Row 4: Rib 76 [76: 80: 80: 84], wrap next st (by slipping next st from left needle onto right needle, taking yarn to opposite side of work between needles and then slipping same st back onto left needle – when working back across wrapped sts work the wrapping loop and the wrapped st together) and turn.
Row 5: Rib 68 [68: 72: 72: 76], wrap next st and turn.
Row 6: Rib 63 [63: 67: 67: 71], wrap next st and turn.
Row 7: Rib 58 [58: 62: 62: 66], wrap next st and turn.
Row 8: Rib 53 [53: 57: 57: 61], wrap next st and turn.
Row 9: Rib 48 [48: 52: 52: 56], wrap next st and turn.
Row 10: Rib 43 [43: 47: 47: 51], wrap next st and turn.
Row 11: Rib 38 [38: 42: 42: 46], wrap next st and turn.
Row 12: Rib 33 [33: 37: 37: 41], wrap next st and turn.
Row 13: Rib 28 [28: 32: 32: 36], wrap next st and turn.
Row 14: Rib to end.
Cont in rib across all sts until collar meas 14 cm at centre back neck.
Cast off in rib.

Button covers (make 2)

Using 6.00mm (US J10) crochet hook and leaving a long end, make 3 ch and join with a ss to form a ring.
Round 1: 1 ch (does NOT count as st), 9 dc into ring, ss to first dc. 9 sts.
Round 2: 1 ch (does NOT count as st), 2 dc into first dc, *1 ch, 2 dc into next dc, rep from * to end, 1 dc into first dc. 27 sts.
Round 3: 3 ch (counts as first tr), 1 tr into "ch sp" formed by dc at end of previous round, *1 ch, miss 2 dc, 2 tr into next ch sp, rep from * to end, 1 ch, ss to top of 3 ch at beg of round.
Fasten off, leaving a long end.
Coil up end of yarn left at start of cover and leave in centre of cover, then place button over this. Using end of yarn left after fastening off, gather up outer edge to enclose button. Fasten off securely.
See information page for finishing instructions, setting in sleeves using the shallow set-in method. Lay right front over left front so that front opening edges overlap. Attaching buttons through both layers, sew buttons onto right front as in photograph, placing first button 3cm below neck edge and second button 15cm below first.
Neatly slip stitch left front neck edge in place on inside.

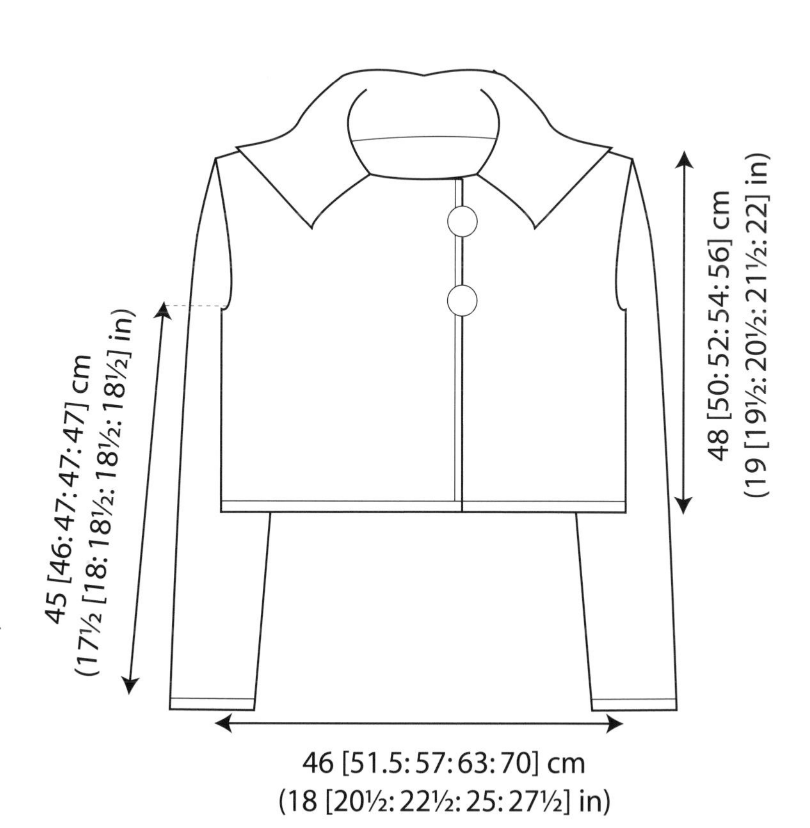

SIZE	S	M	L	XL	XXL	
To fit bust	81-86	91-97	102-107	112-117	122-127	cm
	32-34	36-38	40-42	44-46	48-50	in

YARN
Rowan Cocoon

	S	M	L	XL	XXL	
A Red Wine 819	2	2	2	2	2	x 100gm
B Quarry Tile 818	1	2	2	2	2	x 100gm
C Seascape 813	4	5	5	5	6	x 100gm
D Amber 815	1	1	1	1	1	x 100gm
E Emerald 814	1	2	2	2	2	x 100gm

NEEDLES
1 pair 6mm (no 4) (US 10) needles, 1 pair 7mm (no 2) (US 10½) needles & 6mm (no 4) (US 10) circular needle

TENSION
14 sts and 16 rows to 10 cm measured over st st using 7mm (US 10½) needles.

STRIPE SEQUENCE
Rows 1 to 4: Using yarn A.
Row 5: Using yarn B.
Rows 6 to 11: Using yarn A.
Rows 12 to 17: Using yarn B.
Rows 18 to 20: Using yarn C.
Rows 21 and 22: Using yarn D.
Rows 23 and 24: Using yarn B.
Rows 25 to 32: Using yarn E.
Row 33: Using yarn D.
Rows 34 and 35: Using yarn A.
Row 36: Using yarn B.
Rows 37 to 40: Using yarn A.
Rows 41 to 44: Using yarn B.
Rows 45 to 47: Using yarn D.
Rows 48 and 49: Using yarn C.
Rows 50 and 51: Using yarn B.
Rows 52 to 59: Using yarn E.
Row 60: Using yarn D.
These 60 rows form stripe sequence and are repeated throughout.

BACK
Using 6mm (US 10) needles and yarn C cast on 62 [70: 78: 86: 98] sts.
Row 1 (RS): K2, *P2, K2, rep from * to end.
Row 2: P2, *K2, P2, rep from * to end.
These 2 rows form rib.
Work in rib for a further 14 rows, inc 1 [1: 1: 1: 0] st at each end of last row and ending with RS facing for next row.
64 [72: 80: 88: 98] sts.
Change to 7mm (US 10½) needles.
Beg with a K row and joining in and breaking off colours as required, cont in st st in stripe sequence (see above) as folls:
Cont straight until back meas 49 [50: 51: 52: 53] cm, ending with RS facing for next row.
Shape armholes
Keeping stripes correct, cast off 3 sts at beg of next 2 rows.
58 [66: 74: 82: 92] sts.
Dec 1 st at each end of next 3 [3: 5: 5: 7] rows, then on foll 1 [3: 3: 5: 6] alt rows. 50 [54: 58: 62: 66] sts.
Cont straight until armhole meas 19 [20: 21: 22: 23] cm, ending with RS facing for next row.
Shape back neck and shoulders
Next row (RS): Cast off 4 [5: 5: 6: 7] sts, K until there are 7 [8: 9: 10: 11] sts on right needle and turn, leaving rem sts on a holder.
Work each side of neck separately.
Cast off 3 sts at beg of next row.
Cast off rem 4 [5: 6: 7: 8] sts.
With RS facing, rejoin appropriate yarn to rem sts, cast off centre 28 [28: 30: 30: 30] sts, K to end.
Complete to match first side, reversing shapings.

FRONT
Work as given for back until 30 rows less have been worked than on back to beg of armhole shaping, ending with RS facing for next row.
Divide for neck
Next row (RS): K32 [36: 40: 44: 49] and turn, leaving rem sts on a holder.
Work each side of neck separately.
Keeping stripes correct, dec 1 st at neck edge of 2nd and foll 6 [5: 7: 6: 5] alt rows, then on 3 [4: 3: 3: 4] foll 4th rows.
22 [26: 29: 34: 39] sts.
Work 3 [1: 1: 3: 1] rows, ending with RS facing for next row.
Shape armhole
Keeping stripes correct, cast off 3 sts at beg and dec 1 [0: 0: 1: 0] st at end of next row. 18 [23: 26: 30: 36] sts.
Work 1 row.
Dec 1 st at armhole edge of next 3 [3: 5: 5: 7] rows, then on foll 1 [3: 3: 5: 6] alt rows **and at same time** dec 1 st at neck edge of 3rd [next: next: 3rd: next] and 0 [2: 2: 3: 4] foll 4th rows. 13 [14: 15: 16: 18] sts.

Dec 1 st at neck edge **only** on 2nd [4th: 2nd: 4th: 2nd] and 4 [3: 3: 2: 2] foll 4th rows. 8 [10: 11: 13: 15] sts.
Cont straight until front matches back to beg of shoulder shaping, ending with RS facing for next row.

Shape shoulder

Cast off 4 [5: 5: 6: 7] sts at beg of next row.
Work 1 row.
Cast off rem 4 [5: 6: 7: 8] sts.
With RS facing, rejoin appropriate yarn to rem sts, K to end.
Complete to match first side, reversing shapings.

SLEEVES

Using 6mm (US 10) needles and yarn C cast on 26 [30: 30: 30: 34] sts.
Work in rib as given for back for 12 rows, inc 1 [0: 0: 1: 0] st at each end of last row and ending with RS facing for next row.
28 [30: 30: 32: 34] sts.
Change to 7mm (US 10½) needles.
Beg with a K row, work in st st, shaping sides by inc 1 st at each end of 3rd and foll 1 [1: 2: 2: 2] alt rows, then on every foll 4th row until there are 56 [58: 60: 62: 64] sts.
Cont straight until sleeve meas 45 [46: 47: 47: 47] cm, ending with RS facing for next row.

Shape top

Cast off 3 sts at beg of next 2 rows. 50 [52: 54: 56: 58] sts.
Dec 1 st at each end of next 5 rows, then on every foll alt row until 36 sts rem, then on foll 5 rows, ending with RS facing for next row.
26 sts.
Cast off 6 sts at beg of next 2 rows.
Cast off rem 14 sts.

MAKING UP

Press as described on the information page.
Join both shoulder seams using back stitch, or mattress stitch if preferred.

Neckband

With RS facing, using 6mm (US 10) circular needle and yarn C, pick up and knit 61 [65: 65: 65: 69] sts down left side of neck, place marker on needle, pick up and knit 61 [65: 65: 65: 69] sts up right side of neck, then 34 [34: 38: 38: 38] sts from back.
156 [164: 168: 168: 176] sts.
Round 1 (RS): *K2, P2, rep from * to end.
This round sets position of rib as given for back.
Round 2: Rib to within 2 sts of marker, K2tog, slip marker onto right needle, sl 1, K1, psso, rib to end.
Rep last round 5 times more. 144 [152: 156: 156: 164] sts.
Cast off in rib, still decreasing either side of marker as before.
See information page for finishing instructions, setting in sleeves using the set-in method.

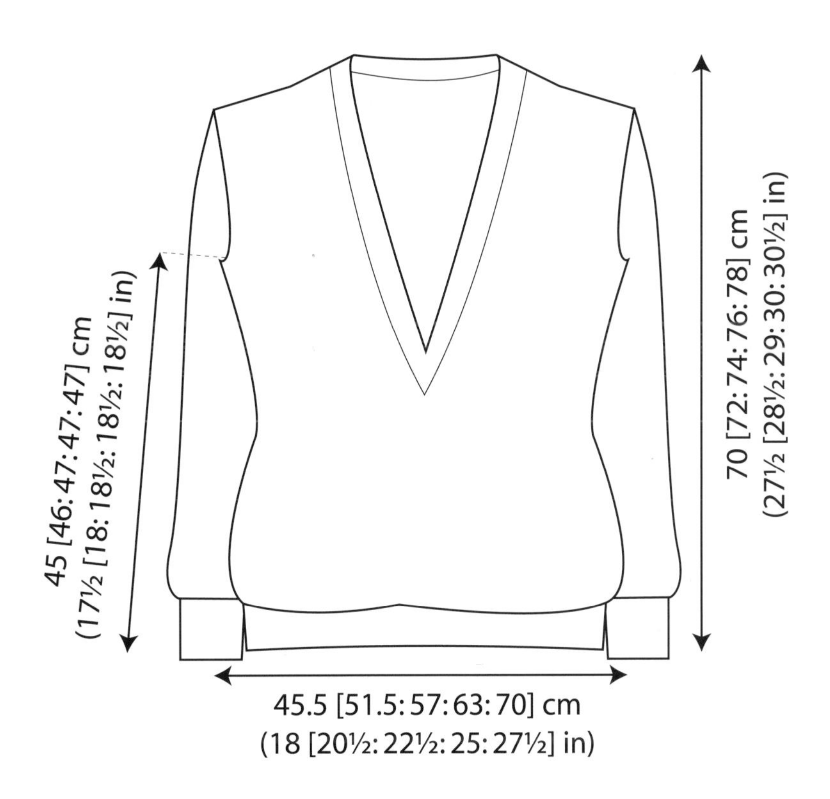

SIZE

	S	M	L	XL	XXL	
To fit bust						
	81-86	91-97	102-107	112-117	122-127	cm
	32-34	36-38	40-42	44-46	48-50	in

YARN

Rowan Cocoon

6	6	7	7	8	x 100gm

(photographed in Cloud 817)

NEEDLES

1 pair 6mm (no 4) (US 10) needles, 1 pair 7mm (no 2) (US 10½) needles & 7mm (no 2) (US 10½) circular needle

TENSION

14 sts and 16 rows to 10 cm measured over st st using 7mm (US 10½) needles.

BACK

Using 6mm (US 10) needles cast on 70 [78: 86: 94: 106] sts.

Row 1 (RS): K2, *P2, K2, rep from * to end.

Row 2: P2, *K2, P2, rep from * to end.

These 2 rows form rib.

Work in rib for a further 20 rows, inc [inc: inc: inc: dec] 1 st at end of last row and ending with RS facing for next row.

71 [79: 87: 95: 105] sts.

Change to 7mm (US 10 1/2) needles.

Beg with a K row, work in st st until back meas 30 [31: 32: 33: 34] cm, ending with RS facing for next row.

Shape raglan armholes

Cast off 3 sts at beg of next 2 rows. 65 [73: 81: 89: 99] sts.

S only

Next row (RS): K1, sl 1, K1, psso, K to last 3 sts, K2tog, K1.

Work 3 rows.

Rep last 4 rows twice more. 59 sts.

L, XL and XXL only

Next row (RS): K1, sl 1, K1, psso, K to last 3 sts, K2tog, K1.

Next row: P1, P2tog, P to last 3 sts, P2tog tbl, P1.

Rep last 2 rows – [-: 2: 5: 8] times more. – [-: 69: 65: 63] sts.

All sizes

Next row (RS): K1, sl 1, K1, psso, K to last 3 sts, K2tog, K1.

Next row: Purl.

Rep last 2 rows 14 [21: 19: 17: 15] times more, ending with RS facing for next row.

Cast off rem 29 [29: 29: 29: 31] sts.

FRONT

Work as given for back until 45 [45: 47: 47: 51] sts rem in raglan armhole shaping.

Work 1 row, ending with RS facing for next row.

Shape neck

Next row (RS): K1, sl 1, K1, psso, K11 [11: 13: 13: 15] and turn, leaving rem sts on a holder.

Work each side of neck separately.

Keeping raglan armhole decreases correct, dec 1 st at raglan armhole edge of 2nd and foll 2 [2: 3: 3: 4] alt rows **and at same time** dec 1 st at neck edge of next 6 rows, then on foll 0 [0: 1: 1: 2] alt rows.

4 sts.

Work 1 row, ending with RS facing for next row.

Next row (RS): K1, sl 1, K2tog, psso.

Next row: P2.

Next row: K2tog and fasten off.

With RS facing, rejoin yarn to rem sts, cast off centre 17 [17: 15: 15: 15] sts, K to last 3 sts, K2tog, K1.

Complete to match first side, reversing shapings.

SLEEVES

Using 6mm (US 10) needles cast on 58 [58: 62: 62: 66] sts.

Work in rib as given for back for 6 rows, dec [inc: dec: inc: dec] 1 st at end of last row and ending with RS facing for next row.

57 [59: 61: 63: 65] sts.

Change to 7mm (US 10½) needles.

Beg with a K row, work in st st, shaping sides by inc 1 st at each end of 3rd and 2 foll 4th rows, then on foll 6th row.

65 [67: 69: 71: 73] sts.

Cont straight until sleeve meas 18 cm, ending with RS facing for next row.

Shape raglan

Cast off 3 sts at beg of next 2 rows. 59 [61: 63: 65: 67] sts.

Working all raglan decreases in same way as back raglan armhole decreases, dec 1 st at each end of next and every foll alt row until 23 sts rem.

Work 1 row, ending with RS facing for next row.

Left sleeve only

Dec 1 st at each end of next row, then cast off 4 sts at beg of foll

row. 17 sts.
Dec 1 st at beg of next row, then cast off 5 sts at beg of foll row. 11 sts.
Rep last 2 rows once more.

Right sleeve only

Cast off 5 sts at beg and dec 1 st at end of next row. 17 sts.
Work 1 row.
Rep last 2 rows twice more.

Both sleeves

Cast off rem 5 sts.

MAKING UP

Press as described on the information page.
Join all raglan seams using back stitch, or mattress stitch if preferred.

Collar

With RS facing and using 7mm (US 10½) circular needle, beg and ending at top of left back raglan seam, pick up and knit 20 sts from top of left sleeve, 10 [10: 12: 12: 14] sts down left side of neck, 17 [17: 15: 15: 15] sts from front, 10 [10: 12: 12: 14] sts up right side of neck, 20 sts from top of right sleeve, then 29 [29: 29: 29: 31] sts from back. 106 [106: 108: 108: 114] sts.
Round 1 (RS of body, WS of collar): Purl.
Rep this round until collar meas 16 cm.
Next round: *K1, P1, rep from * to end.
Rep last round twice more.
Cast off in rib.
See information page for finishing instructions.

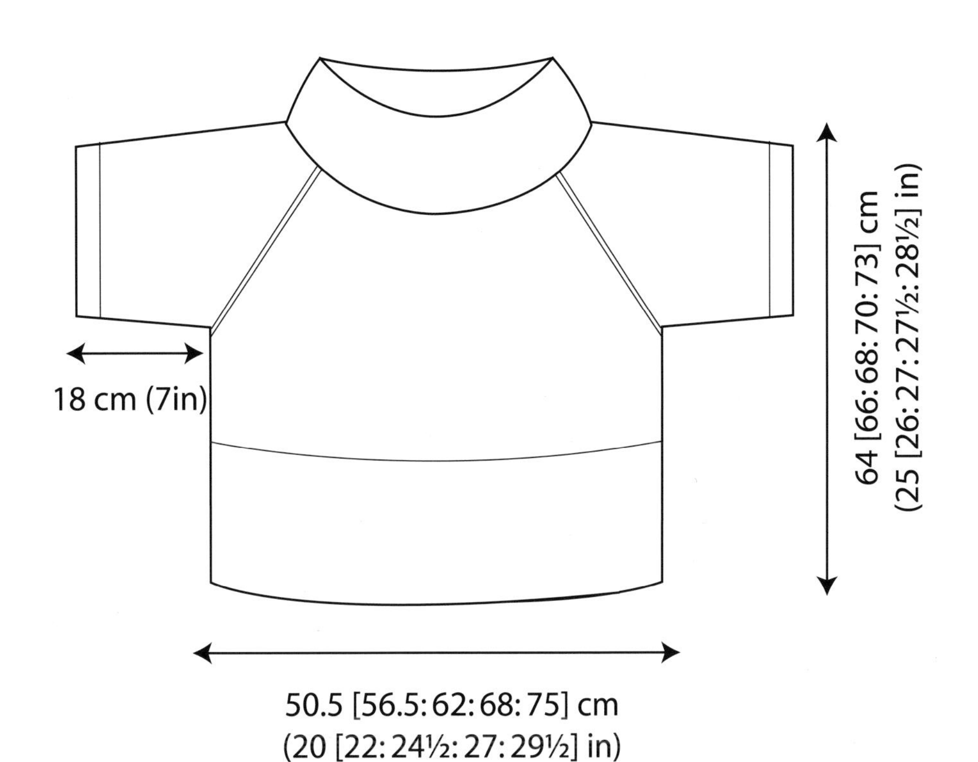

SIZE	S	M	L	XL	XXL	
To fit bust	81-86	91-97	102-107	112-117	122-127	cm
	32-34	36-38	40-42	44-46	48-50	in

YARN
Rowan Cocoon
Round neck sweater

	6	6	7	7	8	x 100gm

(photographed in Kiwi 816)
V neck sweater

	5	6	7	7	8	x 100gm

(photographed in Amber 815)

NEEDLES
1 pair 6mm (no 4) (US 10) needles
1 pair 7mm (no 2) (US 10½) needles

TENSION
14 sts and 16 rows to 10 cm measured over st st using 7mm (US 10½) needles.

MOTIF (9 sts)
Row 1 (RS): K2, K2tog, yfwd, K1, yfwd, K2tog tbl, K2.
Row 2: P9.
Row 3: K1, K2tog, yfwd, K3, yfwd, K2tog tbl, K1.
Row 4: P9.
Row 5: K2tog, yfwd, K5, yfwd, K2tog tbl.
Row 6: P9.
Row 7: K9.
Row 8: P9.
Row 9: K5, insert right needle point into first eyelet hole of row 5 and draw loop through, insert right needle point into first eyelet hole of row 3 and draw loop through, insert right needle point into first eyelet hole of row 1 and draw loop through, insert right needle point into 2nd eyelet hole of row 1 and draw loop through, insert right needle point into 2nd eyelet hole of row 3 and draw loop through, insert right needle point into 2nd eyelet hole of row 5 and draw loop through (6 loops in total), K4.
Row 10: P4, P tog the 6 loops and the next st, P4.
These 10 rows complete the motif.

Round neck sweater

BACK
Using 6mm (US 10) needles cast on 65 [73: 81: 89: 99] sts.
Row 1 (RS): K1, *P1, K1, rep from * to end.
Row 2: P1, *K1, P1, rep from * to end.
These 2 rows form rib.
Work in rib for a further 4 rows, ending with RS facing for next row.
Change to 7mm (US 10½) needles.
Beg with a K row, work in st st for 2 rows, ending with RS facing for next row.
Place motifs
Next row (RS): K2, sl 1, K1, psso (for side seam dec), K6 [4: 2: 6: 5], work next 9 sts as row 1 of motif, (K3, work next 9 sts as row 1 of motif) 3 [4: 5: 5: 6] times, K6 [4: 2: 6: 5], K2tog (for side seam dec), K2. 63 [71: 79: 87: 97] sts.
Next row: P9 [7: 5: 9: 8], work next 9 sts as row 2 of motif, (P3, work next 9 sts as row 2 of motif) 3 [4: 5: 5: 6] times, P9 [7: 5: 9: 8].
These 2 rows set the sts – 4 [5: 6: 6: 7] motifs with st st between and at sides.
Working all side seam decreases as set by first of last 2 rows and keeping motifs correct, dec 1 st at each end of 3rd and foll 4th row. 59 [67: 75: 83: 93] sts.
Work 1 row, ending after motif row 10 and with RS facing for next row.
Beg with a K row, now work all sts in st st and cont as folls:
Work 2 rows.
Working decreases as set, dec 1 st at each end of next row. 57 [65: 73: 81: 91] sts.
Work 13 rows, ending with RS facing for next row.
Next row (inc) (RS): K3, M1, K to last 3 sts, M1, K3.
Work 7 rows, then rep the inc row again. 61 [69: 77: 85: 95] sts.
Cont straight until back meas 35 [36: 37: 38: 39] cm, ending with RS facing for next row.
Shape armholes
Cast off 3 sts at beg of next 2 rows. 55 [63: 71: 79: 89] sts.**
Next row (RS): K2, sl 1, K1, psso, K to last 4 sts, K2tog, K2.
Next row: P2, (P2tog) 0 [1: 1: 1: 1] times, P to last 0 [4: 4: 4: 4] sts, (P2tog tbl, P2) 0 [1: 1: 1: 1] times.
These 2 rows set armhole decreases.
Working all armhole decreases as set by last 2 rows, dec 1 st at each end of next 1 [1: 3: 5: 7] rows, then on foll 1 [3: 2: 2: 3] alt rows. 49 [51: 57: 61: 65] sts.
Cont straight until armhole meas 21 [22: 23: 24: 25] cm, ending with RS facing for next row.
Shape shoulders and back neck
Next row (RS): Cast off 5 [6: 7: 8: 9] sts, K until there are 9 [9: 10: 11: 12] sts on right needle and turn, leaving rem sts on a holder.
Work each side of neck separately.

Cast off 3 sts at beg of next row.
Cast off rem 6 [6: 7: 8: 9] sts.
With RS facing, rejoin yarn to rem sts, cast off centre 21 [21: 23: 23: 23] sts, K to end.
Complete to match first side, reversing shapings.

FRONT
Work as given for back to ★★.
Working all armhole decreases as set by back, dec 1 st at each end of next 1 [3: 5: 7: 9] rows, then on foll 2 [3: 2: 1: 0] alt rows. 49 [51: 57: 63: 71] sts.
Work 5 [1: 1: 1: 1] rows, ending with RS facing for next row.
Shape neck
Next row (RS): (K2, sl 1, K1, psso) 0 [0: 0: 1: 1] times, K18 [19: 21: 20: 24] and turn, leaving rem sts on a holder.
Work each side of neck separately.
Dec 1 st at neck edge of next 4 rows, then on foll 3 alt rows **and at same time** dec 0 [0: 0: 0: 1] st at armhole edge of 2nd and foll alt row. 11 [12: 14: 16: 18] sts.
Cont straight until front matches back to beg of shoulder shaping, ending with RS facing for next row.
Shape shoulder
Cast off 5 [6: 7: 8: 9] sts at beg of next row.
Work 1 row.
Cast off rem 6 [6: 7: 8: 9] sts.
With RS facing, rejoin yarn to rem sts, cast off centre 13 [13: 15: 15: 15] sts, K to last 0 [0: 0: 4: 4] sts, (K2tog, K2) 0 [0: 0: 1: 1] times.
Complete to match first side, reversing shapings.

SLEEVES
Using 6mm (US 10) needles cast on 29 [29: 31: 31: 33] sts.
Work in rib as given for back for 4 rows, ending with RS facing for next row.
Change to 7mm (US 10½) needles.
Beg with a K row, work in st st, shaping sides by inc 1 st at each end of 3rd and every foll 4th row to 33 [37: 39: 45: 47] sts, then on every foll 6th row until there are 51 [53: 55: 57: 59] sts.
Cont straight until sleeve meas 46 [47: 48: 48: 48] cm, ending with RS facing for next row.
Shape top
Cast off 3 sts at beg of next 2 rows. 45 [47: 49: 51: 53] sts.
Dec 1 st at each end of next 5 rows, then on every foll alt row to 27 sts, then on foll 3 rows, ending with RS facing for next row. 21 sts.
Cast off 4 sts at beg of next 2 rows.
Cast off rem 13 sts.

MAKING UP
Press as described on the information page.
Join right shoulder seam using back stitch, or mattress stitch if preferred.
Neckband
With RS facing and using 6mm (US 10) needles, pick up and knit 20 [22: 22: 24: 26] sts down left side of neck, 13 [13: 15: 15: 15] sts from front, 20 [22: 22: 24: 26] sts up right side of neck, then 28 [28: 30: 30: 30] sts from back. 81 [85: 89: 93: 97] sts.
Beg with row 2, work in rib as given for back for 4 rows, ending with **WS** facing for next row.
Cast off in rib (on **WS**).
See information page for finishing instructions.

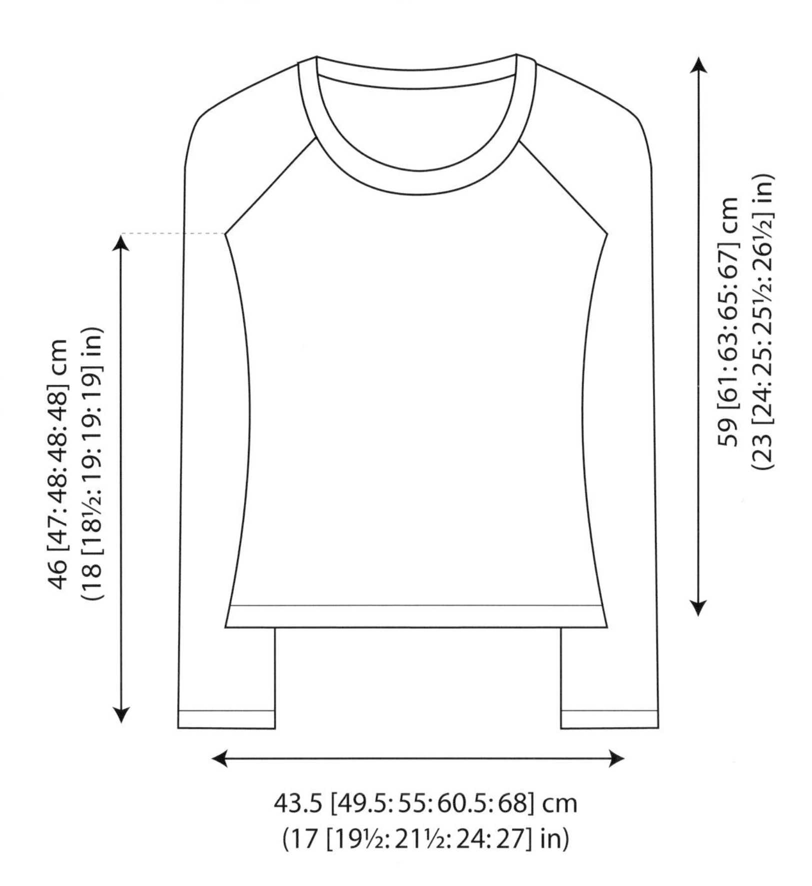

V neck sweater

BACK
Work as given for back of round neck sweater.

FRONT
Work as given for back of round neck sweater to ★★.
Working all armhole decreases as set by back, dec 1 st at each end of next 1 [2: 2: 2: 2] rows. 53 [59: 67: 75: 85] sts.
Work 1 [0: 0: 0: 0] row, ending with RS facing for next row.
Divide for neck
Next row (RS): K2, sl 1, K1, psso, K20 [23: 27: 31: 36], K2tog and turn, leaving rem sts on a holder.
Work each side of neck separately.
Dec 1 st at neck edge of 2nd and foll 11 [10: 12: 11: 10] alt rows, then on 0 [1: 0: 1: 2] foll 4th rows **and at same time** dec 1 st at armhole edge of 2nd [2nd: next: next: next] and foll 0 [0: 1: 3: 5] rows, then on foll 0 [2: 2: 2: 3] alt rows. 11 [12: 14: 16: 18] sts.
Cont straight until front matches back to beg of shoulder shaping, ending with RS facing for next row.
Shape shoulder
Cast off 5 [6: 7: 8: 9] sts at beg of next row.

Work 1 row.
Cast off rem 6 [6: 7: 8: 9] sts.
With RS facing, slip centre st onto a holder, rejoin yarn to rem sts, K2tog, K to last 4 sts, K2tog, K2.
Complete to match first side, reversing shapings.

SLEEVES
Work as given for sleeves of round neck sweater.

MAKING UP
Press as described on the information page.
Join right shoulder seam using back stitch, or mattress stitch if preferred.
Neckband
With RS facing and using 6mm (US 10) needles, pick up and knit 31 [33: 33: 35: 37] sts down left side of neck, K st left on holder at base of V and mark this st with a coloured thread, pick up and knit 31 [33: 33: 35: 37] sts up right side of neck, then 28 [28: 30: 30: 30] sts from back. 93 [95: 97: 101: 105] sts.
Beg with row 2, work in rib as given for back for 1 row, ending with RS facing for next row.
This row sets position of rib.
Keeping rib correct, cont as folls:
Row 2 (RS): Rib to within 1 st of marked st, slip 2 sts as though to K2tog (marked st is 2nd of these 2 sts), K1, pass 2 slipped sts over, rib to end.
Row 3: Rib to marked st, P marked st, rib to end.
Row 4: As row 2.
Cast off in rib (on WS).
See information page for finishing instructions.

YARN
Rowan Cocoon1 x 100gm
(photographed in 813 Seascape)

NEEDLES
1 pair 5.5mm (no 5) (US 9) needles
1 pair 6.5mm (no 3) (US 10fi) needles

TENSION
15 sts and 17 rows to 10cm measured over st st using 6.5mm (US 10fi) needles.

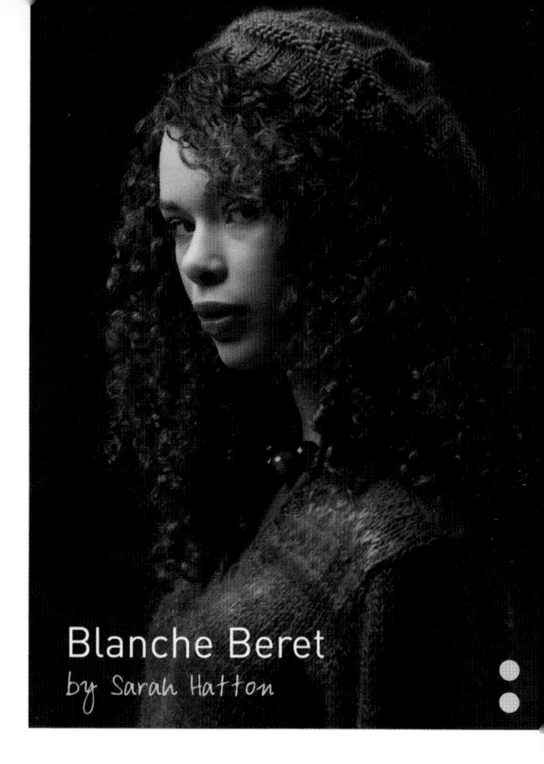

Using 5.5mm (US 9) needles cast on 71 sts.
Row 1 (RS): K1, * yfwd, K2tog, rep from * to end.
Row 2: P1, * K1, P1, rep from * to end.
Row 3: * K1, P1, rep from * to last st, K1.
Rep last 2 rows once.
Next row (WS): Purl.
Change to 6.5mm (US 10 fi) needles.
Next row (RS): K2, * M1, K2, M1, K3, rep from * to last 4 sts, M1, K2, M1, K2. 99 sts.
Starting with P row, work 3 rows in st st, ending with RS facing for next row.
Next row (RS): Purl.
Next row: Knit.
Next row: K1, * yfwd, K3, sl, K1, psso, yfwd, sl, K2tog, psso, yfwd, K2tog, K3, yfwd, K1, rep from * to end.
Next row: Purl.
Rep last 2 rows once.
Next row: Purl.
Knit 2 rows, ending with WS facing for next row.
Next row (WS): P3, * M1, P4, rep from * to end. 123 sts.
Starting with a K row, working in st st throughout, work 6 rows, ending with RS facing for next row.

Shape crown
Row 1 (RS): K6, * sl 2, K1, p2sso, K9, rep from * to last 9 sts, sl 2, K1, p2sso, K6. 103 sts.
Work 3 rows.
Row 5: K5, * sl 2, K1, p2sso, K7, rep from * to last 8 sts, sl 2, K1, p2sso, K5. 83 sts.
Work 3 rows.
Row 9: K4, * sl 2, K1, p2sso, K5, rep from * to last 7 sts, sl 2, K1, p2sso, K4. 63 sts.
Work 3 rows.
Row 13: K3, * sl 2, K1, p2sso, K3, rep from * to last 6 sts, sl 2, K1, p2sso, K3. 43 sts.
Work 3 rows.
Row 17: K2, * sl 2, K1, p2sso, K1, rep from * to last 5 sts, sl 2, K1, p2sso, K2. 23 sts.
Next row: P2tog to last st, P1. 12 sts.
Break yarn and thread through rem 12sts. Pull up tight and fasten off securely.
Join back seam.

MAKING UP
Press as described on the information page.

information

Tension

Obtaining the correct tension is perhaps the single factor which can make the difference between a successful garment and a disastrous one. It controls both the shape and size of an article, so any variation, however slight, can distort the finished garment.
Different designers feature in our books and it is their tension, given at the start of each pattern, which you must match. We recommend that you knit a square in pattern and/or stocking stitch (depending on the pattern instructions) of perhaps
5 - 10 more stitches and 5 - 10 more rows than those given in the tension note. Mark out the central 10cm square with pins. If you have too many stitches to 10cm try again using thicker needles, if you have too few stitches to 10cm try again using finer needles. Once you have achieved the correct tension your garment will be knitted to the measurements indicated in the size diagram shown at the end of the pattern.

Sizing & Size Diagram Note

The instructions are given for the smallest size. Where they vary, work the figures in brackets for the larger sizes. One set of figures refers to all sizes. Included with most patterns in this magazine is a 'size diagram', or sketch of the finished garment and its dimensions. To help you choose the size of garment to knit please refer to the NEW sizing guide on page 102.

Chart Note

Many of the patterns in the book are worked from charts. Each square on a chart represents a stitch and each line of squares a row of knitting. Each colour used is given a different letter and these are shown in the materials section, or in the key alongside the chart of each pattern. When working from the charts, read odd rows (K) from right to left and even rows (P) from left to right, unless otherwise stated. When working lace from a chart it is important to note that all but the largest size may have to alter the first and last few stitches in order not to lose or gain stitches over the row.

Working a Lace Pattern

When working a lace pattern it is important to remember that if you are unable to work both the increase and corresponding decrease and vica versa, the stitches should be worked in stocking stitch.

Knitting With Colour

There are two main methods of working colour into a knitted fabric: Intarsia and Fairisle techniques. The first method produces a single thickness of fabric and is usually used where a colour is only required in a particular area of a row and does not form a repeating pattern across the row, as in the fairisle technique.

Intarsia: The simplest way to do this is to cut short lengths of yarn for each motif or block of colour used in a row. Then joining in the various colours at the appropriate point on the row, link one colour to the next by twisting them around each other where they meet on the wrong side to avoid gaps. All ends can then either be darned along the colour join lines, as each motif is completed or then can be " knitted-in" to the fabric of the knitting as each colour is worked into the pattern. This is done in much the same way as"weaving- in" yarns when working the Fairisle technique and does save time darning-in ends. It is essential that the tension is noted for Intarsia as this may vary from the stocking stitch if both are used in the same pattern.

Fair isle type knitting: When two or three colours are worked repeatedly across a row, strand the yarn not in use loosely behind the stitches being worked. If you are working with more than two colours, treat the "floating" yarns as if they were one yarn and always spread the stitches to their correct width to keep them elastic. It is advisable not to carry the stranded or "floating" yarns over more than three stitches at a time, but to weave them under and over the colour you are working.
The "floating" yarns are therefore caught at the back of the work.

Finishing Instructions

After working for hours knitting a garment, it seems a great pity that many garments are spoiled because such little care is taken in the pressing and finishing process. Follow the following tips for a truly professional-looking garment.

Pressing

Block out each piece of knitting and following the instructions on the ball band press the garment pieces, omitting the ribs. Tip: Take special care to press the edges, as this will make sewing up both easier and neater. If the ball band indicates that the fabric is not to be pressed, then covering the blocked out fabric with a damp white cotton cloth and leaving it to stand will have the desired effect. Darn in all ends neatly along the selvage edge or a colour join, as appropriate.

Stitching

When stitching the pieces together, remember to
match areas of colour and texture very carefully where they meet. Use a seam stitch such as back stitch or mattress stitch for all main knitting seams and join all ribs and neckband with mattress stitch, unless otherwise stated.

Construction

Having completed the pattern instructions, join left shoulder and neckband seams as detailed above. Sew the top of the sleeve to the body of the garment using the method detailed in the pattern, referring to the appropriate guide:

Straight cast-off sleeves: Place centre of cast-off edge of sleeve to shoulder seam. Sew top of sleeve to body, using markers as guidelines where applicable.

Square set-in sleeves: Place centre of cast-off edge of sleeve to shoulder seam. Set sleeve head into armhole, the straight sides at top of sleeve to form a neat right-angle to cast-off sts at armhole on back and front.

Shallow set-in sleeves: Place centre of cast off edge of sleeve to shoulder seam. Match decreases at beg of armhole shaping to decreases at top of sleeve. Sew sleeve head into armhole, easing in shapings.

Set- in sleeves: Place centre of cast-off edge of sleeve to shoulder seam. Set in sleeve, easing sleeve head into armhole.

Join side and sleeve seams.
Slip stitch pocket edgings and linings into place.
Sew on buttons to correspond with buttonholes.
Ribbed welts and neckbands and any areas of garter stitch should not be pressed.

abbreviations & experience ratings

K	knit
P	purl
st(s)	stitch(es)
inc	increas(e)(ing)
dec	decreas(e)(ing)
st st	stocking stitch (1 row K, 1 row P)
g st	garter stitch (K every row)
beg	begin(ning)
foll	following
rem	remain(ing)
rev st st	reverse stocking stitch (1 row K , 1 row P)
rep	repeat
alt	alternate
cont	continue
patt	pattern
tog	together
mm	millimetres
cm	centimetres
in(s)	inch(es)
RS	right side
WS	wrong side
sl 1	slip one stitch
psso	pass slipped stitch over
p2sso	pass 2 slipped stitches over
tbl	through back of loop
M1	make one stitch by picking up horizontal loop before next stitch and knitting into back of it
M1P	make one stitch by picking up horizontal loop before next stitch and purling into back of it
yfwd	yarn forward
yrn	yarn round needle
meas	measures
0	no stitches, times or rows
-	no stitches, times or rows for that size
yo	yarn over needle
yfrn	yarn forward round needle
wyib	with yarn at back

Crochet Terms

UK crochet terms and abbreviations have been used throughout.
The list below gives the US equivalent where they vary.

Abbrev.	UK	US
dc	double crochet	single crochet

Easy, straight forward knitting

Suitable for the average knitter

For the more experienced knitter

sizing guide

Our sizing now conforms to standard clothing sizes.Therefore if you buy a standard size 12 in clothing, then our size 12 or Medium patterns will fit you perfectly.

Dimensions in the charts shown are body measurements, not garment dimensions, therefore please refer to the measuring guide to help you to determine which is the best size for you to knit.

CASUAL SIZING GUIDE FOR WOMEN

As there are some designs that are intended to fit more generously, we have introduced our casual sizing guide.The designs that fall into this group can be recognised by the size range: Small, Medium, Large & Xlarge. Each of these sizes cover two sizes from the standard sizing guide, ie. Size S will fit sizes 8/10, size M will fit sizes 12/14 and so on.

The sizing within this chart is also based on the larger size within the range, ie. M will be based on size 14.

UK SIZE DUAL SIZE	S 8/10	M 12/14	L 16/18	XL 20/22	XXL 24/26	
To fit bust	32 – 34	36 – 38	40 – 42	44 – 46	48 - 50	inches
	82 – 87	92 - 97	102 – 107	112 – 117	122 - 127	cm
To fit waist	24 – 26	28 – 30	32 – 34	36 – 38	40 - 50	inches
	61 – 66	71 – 76	81 – 86	91 – 96	101 - 106	cm
To fit hips	34 – 36	38 – 40	42 – 44	46 – 48	50 - 52	inches
	87 – 92	97 – 102	107 – 112	117 – 122	127 - 132	cm

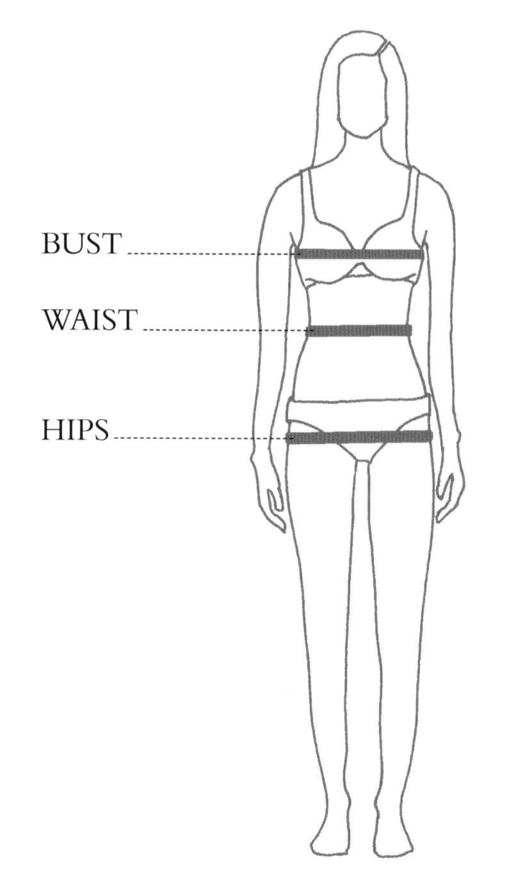

MEASURING GUIDE

For maximum comfort and to ensure the correct fit when choosing a size to knit, please follow the tips below when checking your size. Measure yourself close to your body, over your underwear and don't pull the tape measure too tight!

Bust/chest – measure around the fullest part of the bust/chest and across the shoulder blades.

Waist – measure around the natural waistline, just above the hip bone.

Hips – measure around the fullest part of the bottom.

If you don't wish to measure yourself, note the size of a favourite jumper that you like the fit of. Our sizes are now comparable to the clothing sizes from the major high street retailers, so if your favourite jumper is a size Medium or size 12, then our casual size Medium and standard size 12 should be approximately the same fit.

To be extra sure, measure your favourite jumper and then compare these measurements with the Rowan size diagram given at the end of the individual instructions.

Finally, once you have decided which size is best for you, please ensure that you achieve the tension required for the design you wish to knit.

Remember if your tension is too loose, your garment will be bigger than the pattern size and you may use more yarn. If your tension is too tight, your garment could be smaller than the pattern size and you will have yarn left over.

Furthermore if your tension is incorrect, the handle of your fabric will be too stiff or floppy and will not fit properly. It really does make sense to check your tension before starting every project.

stockists

AUSTRALIA: Australian Country Spinners, 314 Albert Street, Brunswick, Victoria 3056. Tel: (61) 3 9380 3888 Fax: (61) 3 9387 2674
Email: sales@auspinners.com.au

AUSTRIA: Coats Harlander GmbH, Autokaderstrasse 31,
A -1210 Wien. Tel: (01) 27716 – 0 Fax: (01) 27716 - 228

BELGIUM: Coats Benelux, Ring Oost 14A, Ninove, 9400, Belgium
Tel: 0346 35 37 00 Email: sales.coatsninove@coats.com

CANADA: Westminster Fibers Inc, 165 Ledge St, Nashua, NH03060
Tel: (1 603) 886 5041 / 5043 Fax: (1 603) 886 1056
Email: rowan@westminsterfibers.com

CHINA: Coats Shanghai Ltd, No 9 Building , Baosheng Road, Songjiang Industrial Zone, Shanghai.
Tel: (86- 21) 5774 3733 Fax: (86-21) 5774 3768

DENMARK: Coats Danmark A/S, Nannasgade 28, 2200 Kobenhavn N Tel: (45) 35 86 90 50 Fax: (45) 35 82 15 10
Email: info@hpgruppen.dk Web: www.hpgruppen.dk

FINLAND: Coats Opti Oy, Ketjutie 3, 04220 Kerava
Tel: (358) 9 274 871 Fax: (358) 9 2748 7330
Email: coatsopti.sales@coats.com

FRANCE: Coats France / Steiner Frères, SAS 100, avenue du Général de Gaulle, 18 500 Mehun-Sur-Yèvre
Tel: (33) 02 48 23 12 30 Fax: (33) 02 48 23 12 40

GERMANY: Coats GMbH, Kaiserstrasse 1, D-79341 Kenzingen
Tel: (49) 7644 8020 Fax: (49) 7644 802399 Web: www.coatsgmbh.de

HOLLAND: Coats Benelux, Ring Oost 14A, Ninove, 9400, Belgium
Tel: 0346 35 37 00 Email: sales.coatsninove@coats.com

HONG KONG: Coats China Holdings Ltd, 19/F Millennium City 2, 378 Kwun Tong Road, Kwun Tong, Kowloon
Tel: (852) 2798 6886 Fax: (852) 2305 0311

ICELAND: Storkurinn, Laugavegi 59, 101 Reykjavik
Tel: (354) 551 8258 Email: storkurinn@simnet.is

ITALY: Coats Cucirini s.r.l., Via Sarca 223, 20126 Milano
Tel: 800 992377 Fax: 0266111701 Email: servizio.clienti@coats.com

JAPAN: Puppy-Jardin Co Ltd, 3-8-11 Kudanminami Chiyodaku, Hiei Kudan Bldg. 5F, Tokyo Tel: (81) 3 3222-7076 Fax: (81) 3 3222- 7066
Email: info@rowan-jaeger.com

KOREA: Coats Korea Co Ltd, 5F Kuckdong B/D, 935-40 Bangbae- Dong, Seocho-Gu, Seoul Tel: (82) 2 521 6262. Fax: (82) 2 521 5181

LEBANON: y.knot, Saifi Village, Mkhalissiya Street 162, Beirut
Tel: (961) 1 992211 Fax: (961) 1 315553 Email: y.knot@cyberia.net.lb

LUXEMBOURG: Coats Benelux, Ring Oost 14A, Ninove, 9400, Belgium Tel: 054 318989 Email: sales.coatsninove@coats.com

MEXICO: Estambres Crochet SA de CV, Aaron Saenz
1891-7, Monterrey, NL 64650 Mexico Tel: +52 (81) 8335-3870

NEW ZEALAND: ACS New Zealand, 1 March Place, Belfast, Christchurch Tel: 64-3-323-6665 Fax: 64-3-323-6660

NORWAY: Coats Knappehuset AS, Pb 100 Ulset, 5873 Bergen
Tel: (47) 55 53 93 00 Fax: (47) 55 53 93 93

SINGAPORE: Golden Dragon Store, 101 Upper Cross Street #02-51, People's Park Centre, Singapore 058357
Tel: (65) 6 5358454 Fax: (65) 6 2216278 Email: gdscraft@hotmail.com

SOUTH AFRICA: Arthur Bales PTY, PO Box 44644, Linden 2104
Tel: (27) 11 888 2401 Fax: (27) 11 782 6137

SPAIN: Oyambre, Pau Claris 145, 80009 Barcelona.
Tel: (34) 670 011957 Fax: (34) 93 4872672
Email: oyambre@oyambreonline.com

Coats Fabra, Santa Adria
Tel: 932908400 Fax: 932908409 Email: atencion.clientes@coats.com

SWEDEN: Coats Expotex AB, Division Craft, Box 297, 401 24 Goteborg
Tel: (46) 33 720 79 00 Fax: 46 31 47 16 50

SWITZERLAND: Coats Stroppel AG, Stroppelstr.16
CH -5300 Turgi (AG) Tel: (41) 562981220 Fax: (41) 56 298 12 50

TAIWAN: Cactus Quality Co Ltd, P.O.Box 30 485, Taipei, Taiwan, R.O.C., Office: 7FL-2, No 140, Roosevelt Road, Sec 2, Taipei, Taiwan, R.O.C.
Tel: 886-2-23656527 Fax: 886-2-23656503 Email: cqcl@m17.hinet.net

THAILAND: Global Wide Trading, 10 Lad Prao Soi 88, Bangkok 10310 Tel: 00 662 933 9019 Fax: 00 662 933 9110
Email: theneedleworld@yahoo.com

U.S.A.: Westminster Fibers Inc, 165 Ledge St, Nashua, NH03060
Tel: (1 603) 886 5041 / 5043 Fax: (1 603) 886 1056
Email: rowan@westminsterfibers.com

U.K: Rowan, Green Lane Mill, Holmfirth, West Yorkshire, England HD9 2DX
Tel: +44 (0) 1484 681881 Fax: +44 (0) 1484 687920
Email: mail@knitrowan.com Web: www.knitrowan.com

For stockists in all other countries please contact Rowan for details

• Photographer: Moy Williams
• Stylist: Marie Wallin
• Hair & Make-up: Michela Taylor
• Models: Emerald Lewis - Independent Models
• Art Director: Marie Wallin
• Design Layout: Lee Wills & Lisa Richardson

With special thanks to the following handknitters:
Jenny Shore, Pat Garden, Barbara Wiltshire, Susan Grimes, Sandra Richardson, Joyce Limon, Janet Oakey, Joyce Coop, Audrey Kidd, Ann Banks, Elsie Eland, Anne Newton, Teresa Gogay, Julie Ferguson, Honey Ingram, Margaret Oswald & Jean Fletcher

First published in Great Britain in 2008 by Rowan Yarns Ltd, Green Lane Mill, Holmfirth, West Yorkshire, England, HD9 2DX
Internet: www.knitrowan.com

British Library Cataloguing in Publication Data Rowan Yarns - The Cocoon Collection
ISBN 978-1-906007-48-5